Contents

I Economic Overview:
   The Issues of Mrs Thatcher's First Term

Introduction   1

1 Pumping in the anti-freeze   9
2 Overfunding: the hidden cost of monetarism   13
3 The twin dangers that could wreck the welfare state   17
4 Moving to a balanced budget?   21
5 Tax cuts only for some   26
6 Giving state industries room to breathe   29

II Economic Overview:
   The Issues of Mrs Thatcher's Second Term

Introduction   35

1 The June 1983 election: the most uncertain choice   37
2 This time oil must be made to pay   41
3 Proving the pain was worthwhile   44
4 Facing up to the public spending Leviathan   47
5 The black hole in the economy   51

III Inflation and Unemployment

Introduction   54

1 Should we learn to live with inflation?   59
2 Will recovery put paid to lower inflation?   63

3 A hard road back to full employment 68
4 Does cheaper labour mean more jobs? 72
5 Playing the jobless numbers game 77
6 Job schemes: only second best 81

IV Productivity, Competitiveness and Investment

Introduction 87

1 The cost of higher productivity 95
2 Industry needs more than lower interest rates 99
3 Sterling's slide is good news for industry 104

V The International Scene

Introduction 109

1 Make or break for the world economy 113
2 Recovery holds the key to third-world debt 118
3 Why the world wants a slow US recovery 121
4 The growing disillusionment with floating exchange rates 124
5 In search of an anchor for floating currencies 128
6 The temptations of protectionism 132
7 Missing the target on overseas investment 135

Questions 139

1 Economic Overview: The Issues of Mrs Thatcher's First Term

Introduction

The Conservative government came to office in 1979 determined to break with the consensus economic policies of the past. It believed that Keynesian demand management – under which governments undertook to maintain full employment, if necessary by injecting cash into the economy through tax cuts or higher public spending – had been discredited. Each successive economic cycle had been characterised by ever higher inflation *and* unemployment. Each successive injection of demand had less and less impact on output and more and more impact on prices.

But the Conservatives were not the first to adopt 'monetarist' policies – that is, the use of money supply targets to control inflation. Monetary targets were first introduced in 1976 by a Labour Chancellor, Mr Denis Healey, as part of the rescue package mounted by the International Monetary Fund following the sterling crisis that year. Earlier, with the crisis at its height, the Prime Minister, Mr James Callaghan, told the Labour Party Conference that Keynesian policies no longer offered a way through Britain's economic difficulties.

'We used to think that you could spend your way out of a recession and increase employment by cutting taxes and boosting government spending. I tell you, in all candour, that that option no longer exists, and that in so far as it ever did exist, it only worked on each occasion since the war by injecting a bigger dose of inflation into the economy, followed by a higher level of unemployment.'

2 Economic Overview

Higher inflation followed by higher unemployment, he said, was the history of the past 20 years.

It was not the Conservative government's adoption of monetary targets that distinguished it from its predecessors. It was its single-minded pursuit of lower inflation through the sole instrument of monetary control, and its explicit rejection of responsibility for securing full employment.

The Thatcher government's approach to the economy in 1979 was conditioned by three central tenets:

1. The government could not make the economy grow; that was the job of management and workers. It could only provide the right conditions for growth, the foremost of which was low inflation.

2. The way to bring inflation down was to control the money supply, the government's only reliable weapon, using interest rates backed by curbs on public borrowing.

3. The adverse impact on output and jobs would be small and temporary as long as people believed the government would stick to its guns, because they would soon adjust pay claims and pricing policies accordingly. This was the thinking behind the medium-term financial strategy, introduced in the 1980 Budget, with its immutable monetary targets for up to four years ahead.

As the high priest of monetarism, Professor Milton Friedman, told the House of Commons Treasury Select Committee in 1980, 'only a modest reduction in output and employment will be a side effect of reducing inflation to single figures by 1982.'

These textbook precepts proved more difficult to apply in Britain's open and hidebound economy. Ministers soon discovered that controlling monetary expansion was no simple matter. In the first phase, higher interest rates – jacked up from 12 per cent base lending rates at election time to 17 per cent six months later – added to industrial costs, undermining competitiveness, and served to intensify rather than curb money supply growth.

Companies, labouring under the heavier burden of loan costs, turned to the banks for help to stay afloat as the recession deepened. Bank lending, and hence the money supply, soared. In addition, the high interest rates paid by banks on deposits diverted savings from elsewhere, further boosting money growth. And institutional changes, including abolition of the 'corset' on bank lending and the introduction of current accounts paying interest, made the situation worse.

By the autumn of 1980, when jobs were being lost at the rate of 100,000 a month, the Treasury had lost its faith in the efficacy of interest rates to control the money supply. Rates began to come down and their subsequent movements owed a good deal more to the behaviour of the exchange rate than that of monetary growth.

The emphasis switched to reducing government borrowing. This was supposed to help restrain the money supply 'without excessive reliance on interest rates'. The fiscal squeeze, the tightest of any major Western country, undoubtedly played a part in bringing inflation down. But the direct link between state borrowing, the money supply and interest rates has proved tenuous. Rates remain high, especially in real, inflation-adjusted terms.

One reason is that other components of the money supply – such as bank lending – may swamp the effect of lower public borrowing.[1] It also takes time for lenders to adjust their expectations for future inflation, which are largely conditioned by past experience, and alter interest rates accordingly. Government hopes that clear signs of its determination to combat inflation would quickly and decisively shift these expectations have been disappointed.

Perhaps most importantly, the strength of the United States dollar – boosted by high American interest rates which followed the introduction of strict monetarist policies in 1979 – has consistently kept up British rates as the government has tried to prevent the pound falling too far and putting its inflation objectives at risk. In the first four years of Mrs Thatcher's government, monetary targets (despite upward revisions) were met only once, in 1982-83. But inflation, after an initial spurt following the doubling of VAT and steep public sector wage awards, has come down dramatically.

The battle has been waged at considerable cost in lost output and jobs. For the weapon has not been the shifting expectations that the original theory suggested, but a combination of deflationary fiscal and money policies and the unplanned temporary – but still potent – explosion of the sterling exchange rate.

1 See 'Overfunding: the hidden cost of monetarism' on p. 13.

4   Economic Overview

Target Growth for £M3 at Annual Rate %

Budget	1979-80	1980-81	1981-82	1982-83	1983-84	1984-85	1985-86
1980	7-11	7-11	6-10	5-9	4-8		
1981			6-10	5-9	4-8		
1982				8-12	7-11	6-10	
1983					7-11	6-10	5-9
outcome	16¼	19¼	13	11	na	na	na

Source: Bank of England

Between early 1979 and its peak in January 1981, the trading value of the pound, adjusted for international variations in costs and productivity, rose by around 45 per cent. Foreigners poured money into Britain, attracted by its high interest rates, confidence in Mrs Thatcher's tough policies and the rapidly rising value of North Sea oil. This helped the fight against inflation by cheapening the cost of imports and putting pressure on companies to keep wage costs down. Indeed, for one school of monetarism – the international monetarists – this was the principal mechanism through which monetary restraint led to lower inflation. But the corollary was the bankruptcy of much of British manufacturing industry as its goods were priced out of world markets.

In retrospect, the Treasury had to concede that despite the waywardness of the target money measure – sterling M3 – financial conditions were actually very tight during 1980 and much of 1981. It was forced to shift further and further away from the original belief in sacrosanct money targets.

In 1980 there was 'no question of departing from the money supply policy'. By 1983 (a year after two additional target measures of money had been added to sterling M3) this had become:

'The interpretation of monetary conditions will continue to take account of all the available evidence, including the exchange rate, structural changes in financial markets, saving behaviour, and the level and structure of interest rates. Policy decisions will be aimed at maintaining monetary conditions that will keep inflation on a downward trend.'

The problem with so many dials to watch is deciding which to focus on and what to do when they point in different directions. In late 1981 sterling was strong but the money supply was growing well above target. The authorities refused to let interest rates fall. In 1982 in similar circumstances interest rates came down. The discrepancy can be explained by the fact that in 1982 inflation was tumbling and the real economy was still stuck firmly in recession, while in 1981 inflation remained uncomfortably high. But outside observers must now read the minds of ministers and their officials to interpret policy. The old set rules have gone.

In practice, the behaviour of the exchange rate has been by far the most important influence on money policy, guiding many if not most of the government's interest rate decisions since 1981. The government has eschewed a target for sterling – but it certainly has views on what happens to it. It does not want the pound too high, because that hurts competitiveness and retards economic growth. It does not want it too low because this pushes up inflation. Nor does it want the pound to move too quickly in either direction because bandwagon effects in the foreign exchange markets can get out of hand and push the currency too far.

The increased attention paid to the exchange rate reflects a greater appreciation of the permanent damage to the economy that can be inflicted by currency values which bear little or no relation to underlying economic performance. This has led some people to urge a more formal role for sterling in money policy. But ministers still take the view that setting targets for the pound would simply court the attentions of speculators and inhibit the government's freedom of action.

The government's choice between growth and inflation in exchange rate policy is mirrored in its monetary guidelines. Though Mr Nigel Lawson, the Chancellor of the Exchequer, has made clear his determination to keep inflation low and falling, present monetary targets have plainly been subordinated to the needs of recovery.

The 1983-84 target band of 7 to 11 per cent was set to allow plenty of room for growth rather than to reduce inflation further (at the time prices were expected to rise at an average annual rate of about 5.5 per cent over the year), and Mr Lawson's predecessor, Sir Geoffrey Howe, was certainly prepared to allow targets to be overshot rather than jack up interest rates and risk aborting the upturn.

Mr Lawson too may face this choice. Economic recovery could put his targets at risk as companies borrow to finance expansion. In recent years they have increasingly turned to the banks. The Chancellor will be hoping that higher profits and greater recourse to the long-term capital markets as interest rates fall will make extra borrowing from the banks unnecessary. If not, he will have to decide whether to accommodate the expansion or constrain it, with depressing effects on the economy.

In the government's scheme of things fiscal policy plays a subordinate rôle to monetary policy. Fiscal contraction which permits interest rates to be lower than they otherwise would be is not necessarily deflationary, ministers have argued. They believe that, in the long run, economic expansion via lower inflation and interest rates – and so lower costs to industry – will be more sustainable than a reflation fuelled by increased government borrowing which may stoke up inflationary fires.

Critics point out that no predictable link between state borrowing and interest rates has been established – for the reasons discussed earlier – nor have interest rates been shown to have as powerful an effect on economic activity as changes in taxation or public spending. The government has nevertheless steadily reduced its budget deficit each year since 1980-81; it has done so in the face of rising unemployment, which automatically

PSBR as % of GDP

Budget	1979-80	1980-81	1981-82	1982-83	1983-84	1984-85	1985-86
1980	4¾	3¾	3	2¼	1½		
1981			4¼	3¼	2		
1982				3½	2¾	2	
1983					2¾	2½	2
outcome	5	5½	3½	3¼	na	na	na

Source: Treasury

increases social security spending and deprives the Exchequer of tax revenues, by raising taxes to record levels.

Targets for the public sector borrowing requirement (PSBR) have come to assume a central importance, even though the government's record in hitting them is a poor one. This is not surprising. The PSBR is the difference between two very large numbers for government spending and revenue. Only 40 per cent of spending is amenable to strict control through the cash limit system. The rest is determined by the demand for services, such as social security benefits, or is local authority spending only indirectly influenced by government. Revenues are even more unpredictable, with taxes on income and spending both sensitive to what happens to economic growth and inflation.

PSBR forecasts can thus be a misleading guide to government action, with an erroneously high forecast, for instance, leading to perhaps unnecessary tax increases or spending cuts.

Ministers' attempts to reduce public spending have been thwarted by the recession and by the government's pledge to increase budgets for defence and law and order. Planned spending was 7 per cent higher in real terms in 1983-84 than in 1978-79. Increases of more than 20 per cent in defence and social security programmes, which together account for over two-fifths of the total, have outweighed cuts in other areas, notably housing and education.

Public sector investment, which declined by 23 per cent between 1978 and 1982, has been hit disproportionately hard. Housing has suffered the biggest reduction (though part of this is accounted for by receipts from council house sales which appear in the accounts as negative capital spending). But social capital such as hospitals and schools, infrastructure such as roads and sewers, and productive investment by the nationalised industries have all fallen victim to government cutbacks.

Like private companies the state corporations have traditionally borrowed – via the government – to finance investment plans. But ministers have sharply reduced their borrowing limits, arguing once again that higher borrowing (within fixed monetary targets) will push up interest rates and so 'crowd out' investment in the private sector (or necessitate higher taxes or cuts in other government programmes to keep total borrowing down).

The all-party Treasury Select Committee of MPs, however, found no solid evidence for 'crowding out' when they looked into the matter in 1981. While the cost of borrowing is important for investment, it is the prospects for demand which are critical. If restrictions on public borrowing depress the economy, lower interest rates – even if they come about – may not be enough to stimulate private investment. Cutbacks in public investment often fall directly on the private sector by reducing demand for their products. If, on the other hand, higher state borrowing promotes economic expansion the boost to demand may well outweigh the higher cost of credit, as the buoyant 1983 American recovery demonstrates.

The other objection to the Treasury view is that it should not matter whether an investment in the public sector displaces one in the private sector if it has a better rate of return. Ministers counter-attack that in practice much nationalised industry investment has produced poor returns in recent years and no return at all on average. Returns on private investment have also been poor, however – falling to only 3 per cent in the depths of recession – because sluggish growth has likewise held back company revenue.

The government's preferred solution is to let the market decide. It has accordingly embarked on an ambitious programme of privatisation – selling state enterprises to the private sector – as part of its 'supply-side' approach to reinvigorating the economy. It believes that public ownership of itself promotes inefficiency and encourages complacency. This is not simply because a number of state industries command almost impregnable monopoly positions (electricity and water, for example), and are thus bulwarked against market forces, but because public ownership provides a state guarantee against bankruptcy.

In practice, privatisation has not, in general, altered either the nature of the industry or the competitive environment. The 'discipline of market forces' is no more or less than before, though the industry is freed, for good or ill, from government interference.

The spur to efficiency from removing the state guarantee against bankruptcy is also more apparent than real. It is hard to see the government letting British Aerospace, which relies on defence contracts for much of its income, go bust – while there is nothing to prevent a technically bankrupt state industry from ceasing to trade (though it cannot legally cease to exist).

Privatisation also poses a problem of public accountability. The government still holds nearly half the shares in most of the privatised industries, an acknowledged form of public ownership and involvement in other European countries. But the British government has announced that it will not normally use the voting rights to which the ownership of shares entitles it, except to prevent control of the company passing into undesirable hands.

Private owners and management thus have complete freedom to run as they see fit a company in which taxpayers have an important financial stake. There is no mechanism for public or Parliamentary scrutiny of these half-private, half-public companies.

The articles in this section focus on Mrs Thatcher's first term of office, from May 1979 to June 1983. The first article, 'Pumping in the anti-freeze', illustrates the problems of trying to target the PSBR and documents the shift in the government's position from unconcern over the restrictive stance of fiscal policy to realisation that too tight a fiscal stance can screw the economy down.

'Overfunding: the hidden cost of monetarism' explains why high bank lending means reducing the PSBR and may not lead to lower interest rates.

Two pieces on the longer term follow. The background to government fears of a future public spending explosion is discussed in 'The twin dangers that could wreck the welfare state', while 'Moving to a balanced budget?' describes ways of measuring a balanced budget and what they mean for government policy.

The government's failure to reduce the personal tax burden in its first term is reviewed in 'Tax cuts only for some'. Finally, 'Giving state industries room to breathe' looks at the impact of tight borrowing constraints on nationalised enterprises, and discusses some of the arguments for privatisation.

1 Pumping in the anti-freeze

Published November 6 1982

In early November 1982, with a 1983 general election in prospect, the economy was in the doldrums. Instead of the healthy recovery ministers were hoping for, national output had scarcely risen since the previous autumn and unemployment was still climbing steeply.

Two factors were blamed. First, the government's fiscal stance looked tighter than intended, chiefly because local councils were holding back on spending on housing and other capital programmes. Secondly, sterling was very strong, continuing to impair the competitiveness of British industry. On November 5 1982 the pound's effective exchange rate against a basket of leading currencies was, at 92.0 (1975=100), more than 3 per cent above its level a year earlier.

The government's reaction was to exhort town halls to use up their investment budgets and to loosen the reins of monetary policy. In the four months between July and early November 1982 bank base lending rates fell from 12 to 9 per cent.

Was this a policy U-turn, a sign that ministers now placed their faith in reflation to launch the economy into orbit? Or was it, as the article argues, simply an attempt to arrest a tighter than expected squeeze.

Ministers have been striking a number of reflationary matches over the past few months – interest rate cuts, abolition of HP controls, exhortations to councils to spend more on investment. But these matches are not so much warming the chilly water of the British economy as preventing its freezing solid. Ministers have become increasingly alarmed that their tough economic policies, designed to squeeze out inflation, are in danger of throttling the economy altogether.

It is clear that public borrowing in 1982-83 will undershoot the £9,500m target by at least £1,500m and probably more than £2,000m, equivalent to nearly 1 per cent of national output. This means £2,000m less cash going into the economy than the government planned, only partly, if at all, offset by the mild boost to private spending conferred by rapidly falling inflation and lower interest rates.

One of the main reasons for this public borrowing shortfall is the reluctance of local authorities (and to a lesser extent state industries) to spend the money earmarked for capital investment. Councils will probably underspend by more than £1,000m, a third of the total sum allocated for capital projects in 1982-83.

The Issues of Mrs Thatcher's First Term 11

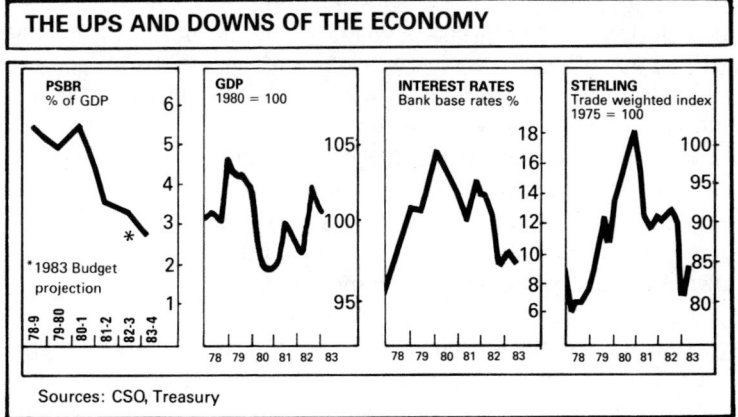

Capital spending, apart from providing and maintaining vital infrastructure needed by the economy, efficiently converts spending into jobs, especially in construction which is now extremely depressed. So it is not surprising that Mrs Thatcher should be so concerned that local authorities spend the money available. They will not, for the simple reason that there is not enough time to put projects in motion before the end of the financial year. And there is not much point in building schools, old people's homes and clinics when continued government restrictions on current spending means councils cannot afford the teachers, nurses and welfare workers to staff them. But telling local authorities to take advantage of the money already allocated to them can hardly be described as an 'expansionary' measure when the government's original spending plans involved a further tightening of budget policy. It is simply a desperate attempt to stop the contraction being even worse.

Since Mrs Thatcher came to power in 1979, the government has determinedly overridden the built-in stabilisers which automatically push up public borrowing in recession through lower tax revenues and extra spending on social security benefits. In 1980 it tightened the screw by the equivalent of 1 per cent of national output, in 1981 by 3.5 per cent and 1982 Budget plans would have involved a further 1.1 per cent contraction. Now it could be greater.

If the government sticks broadly to its medium-term financial strategy, and keeps public borrowing falling as a proportion of national output, budget policy will tighten again in 1983-84. The

£3,000m or so that Sir Geoffrey Howe reportedly has in hand to return in tax cuts or help for industry in the spring will be needed just to prevent policy becoming even more restrictive.

On the face of it, the government's shift to an expansionary monetary policy is much more marked. The Treasury has abandoned its (unsuccessful) attempts to apply rigid targets to a single measure of money growth. Now it claims to look at three money supply measures and the exchange rate, while the target ranges for money growth have been adjusted up rather than down and past overshoots accommodated.

The authorities have been bringing interest rates down quite aggressively and the Chancellor made it clear recently that this process would not stop even if money growth exceeded target.

With monetary expansion at nearly 12 per cent and accelerating, and inflation at 7.3 per cent and falling, money policy looks expansionary. The problem is that it does not feel that way. Officials point to the extraordinary strength of sterling, now higher on balance than a year ago, and the plunging rate of inflation as evidence that underlying monetary conditions remain very tight. Even with the latest fall in interest rates, real rates – adjusted for expected inflation – which are what matter to companies considering investment are still discouragingly high for an economy in the depths of recession. To put up interest rates to choke off rapid money growth would strangle the economy when it is still gasping for breath.

Treasury ministers have come to accept, in a significant departure from their previous crude and deterministic monetarism, that government action is crucial in keeping the economy afloat, and that the private sector will not automatically fill the breaches left by public cutbacks. But to characterise as 'expansionary' the measures that have been taken so far or those now in prospect is a long way from the truth.

Subsequent events took the government and most outside analysts by surprise. A week after this article was written the pound began to slide on world currency markets, falling by 15 per cent to a trough of 78 on its trade weighted index in March 1983. Interest rates jumped to 11 per cent to help stem the drop in sterling.

Public borrowing, which up to the last moment indicated

a massive undershoot on its £9,500m target, finally turned out at £9,200m after an eleventh hour spending spree by government departments (not town halls – despite pleas to spend more).

The economy – helped by the fall in sterling and a looser fiscal stance – picked up smartly, growing at an annual rate of 3.7 per cent between the second half of 1982 and the first half of 1983.

2 Overfunding: the hidden cost of monetarism

Published June 28 1982

In the six months to March 1982 the government lent industry nearly £7bn. That is equivalent to its entire revenues from North Sea oil last year, four-fifths of its total borrowing and seven times the annual budget envisaged by the Labour Party for an aggressively interventionist national investment bank.

Why have we not heard the howls of outraged free enterprise from the Tory backbenches? The accusations of a U-turn? Triumphant gloatings from a vindicated Opposition? The reason is that this lending was made not because ministers chose to aid industry as part of some revamped industrial strategy. It happened as the direct and embarrassing by-product of the government's determination to stick to its monetarist economic policies by trying to hold down money growth in the face of a bank lending explosion.

For the past few weeks some of the best brains in the Treasury and the Bank of England have been pondering how to extricate themselves from this arcane money conundrum known as 'overfunding'. There were high-level fears that unless something was done, they might even face Opposition charges that 'Mrs Thatcher's monetarism' was illegal. On Friday the Chancellor of the Exchequer announced the result of these deliberations.

The problem is this: the government has set targets for the growth of the money supply which it believes will help curb

Economic Overview

inflation. But bank lending to industry and households, one of the principal components of money supply, has in recent months risen by more than the target allows for total money growth. To stick to the money target the other main component – the public sector contribution – must be negative. This is achieved by the government selling more long-term debt – gilts and national savings – to the public (other than banks) than is necessary to finance its own borrowing needs; in other words, it is 'overfunding' its borrowing requirement.

The trouble is that overfunding has repercussions in the short-term money markets where the crucial and politically sensitive interest rates which determine the cost of overdrafts and mortgages are decided. When governments spend money they in effect put cash into the banking system. When they sell gilts or collect taxes they drain cash out of the system (because people pay with money held with the banks). So if the government sells more gilts than it needs to cover the gap between spending and taxes the banking system finds itself short of cash. Left alone, this shortage would result in interest rates being bid up, perhaps to horrendous levels. The government does not want this to happen. So it has been pumping cash back into the system, which it does by buying short-term paper (IOUs), mostly bills issued by companies and held by the banks.

Overfunding the Public Sector Borrowing Requirement

	PSBR £m	Debt sales to non-bank private sector £m	Bank lending to private sector £m	Of which: Bills bought by Bank of England £m	Increase in £M3 £m
1978-79	9,224	8,514	6,296	−101	5,262
1979-80	9,909	9,184	9,330	765	6,443
1980-81	13,191	10,896	9,248	2,015	10,693
1981-82	8,813	11,229	14,928	4,240	9,808
1982-83	9,166	8,196	14,356	−787	10,106

Source: CSO, *Financial Statistics*

In effect, the Bank of England has been lending money to the banks to enable them to go on lending to industry – the very lending that the authorities were trying to offset by overfunding in the first place. The Bank of England has become a gigantic money recycling machine.

The machine was tested almost to destruction in the second half of the 1981-82 financial year. The end of the Civil Service dispute meant huge payments of back taxes on top of the normal taxpaying season. In addition, many companies decided to borrow money from the banks to pay their taxes. The government tried to offset the impact of this on the money supply by selling gilts, thus making the shortages in the money markets even worse. Over that period the Bank of England bought a record £7bn of commercial bills.

The system for operating in the money markets, introduced less than a year ago, was simply not designed to cope with persistent over-funding. The idea was that in months when the government was in surplus the Bank of England would buy bills to relieve money market shortages and in months when it was in deficit (because of low tax revenues or gilt sales) it would sell them back again, roughly evening things out over the year.

Instead, overfunding to hit money targets, because of high bank lending, means the government accounts are more often in surplus than not. So the Bank is accumulating more and more commercial bills and providing more and more finance for industrial lending. This cannot go on indefinitely.

For a start, there is probably a limit to how much companies want to borrow through issuing bills, so the Bank may run out of bills to buy. This is despite the fact that the authorities' need to buy bills has created such favourable terms for them that, according to allegations current in the City (but strongly denied by the Bank), companies have issued bills, not because they need to borrow but so they can deposit the money with the banks at a profit. This has, it is claimed, artificially swelled the bank lending figures and forced the government to do more overfunding, leading to more bill buying and so on in a vicious money circle.

Secondly, the Bank itself faced the possibility of being unable legally to buy in more bills above a certain limit fixed by the liabilities of the Issue Department. These happen to be notes and coin in circulation, the amount of which depends on demand and not on a decision by the Bank.

Thirdly, and most importantly, the system is perverse. Long-term interest rates are higher than they would otherwise be because the government is trying to sell more debt. This not only increases the cost of government borrowing. It discourages companies from borrowing long term because of the high interest they would have to pay to compete with gilts. Instead, they are positively encouraged to borrow short term directly from the banks or through issuing bills (which comes to the same thing), adding yet more fuel to the bank lending explosion.

There are those, in the City and in Whitehall, who believe the problem may go away of its own accord. The huge shortages caused by the unwinding of the Civil Service strike are unlikely to be repeated. And they expect the growth of bank lending to slow down later this year because companies now have plenty of cash and their profits are improving, reducing their borrowing needs. That means the government may not have to overfund to meet monetary targets.

The Treasury is doing its best to ensure overfunding becomes unnecessary. The Chancellor has announced measures designed to divert borrowing away from the banks, by making government loans more attractive for local authorities and other public sector bodies, and by encouraging companies to raise funds in the long-term capital markets through bonds and share issues. He has also proposed changes to remove the constraint on the Bank's ability to buy bills, in time for the next main taxpaying season later this year.

Whether these measures will do the trick remains to be seen. Cutting public sector borrowing will not permit lower interest rates, as the government has repeatedly claimed, if high bank lending continues to put its money targets at risk.

In 1982-83 no overfunding was necessary because the external component of the money supply – which includes bank lending overseas and changes in the official reserves – was strongly negative. This enabled the government to meet its money target despite high bank lending and an underfunded PSBR.

Mr Nigel Lawson, the Chancellor, said in his Mansion House speech in autumn 1983 that the government's objective was broadly to fund the PSBR, neither more nor less, over the medium term. However, there can be no guarantee that the debt sales this implies will be what is needed to keep the money supply on track, which depends very much on what happens to bank lending.

3 The twin dangers that could wreck the welfare state

Published August 3 1982

In the spring of 1982, Treasury ministers kicked off a debate on the outlook for public spending in the longer term, based on internal calculations which suggested an inexorable tendency for spending to grow. The Chancellor and his Chief Secretary, Mr Leon Brittan, urged a radical reappraisal of the welfare state, proposing that the state should confine itself to providing basic services and leave the private sector to satisfy additional demands.

Recent calls by the Chancellor, Sir Geoffrey Howe, and his second-in-command, Mr Leon Brittan, for a bigger private element in public services should not be judged simply as the opening shots in a confined debate about Conservative priorities after the next election, involving a natural extension of the government's existing denationalisation programme.

They have a much wider significance. They mark the first political proposals, albeit based on an unashamedly free-market philosophy, to defuse what many believe to be a costly time bomb ticking under the foundations of the welfare state. That time bomb has two dangerous components: people's apparently insatiable appetite for more and better public services, and unfavourable demographic changes which mean that increasing numbers, especially of old people, will come to depend heavily on the state for support and aid.

The fuse is sluggish economic growth which many fear may persist for years. This means the economy cannot provide sufficient wealth to maintain, let alone improve, public services while leaving more cash in people's pockets to finance higher private living standards. At some point, unless something is done, the tax burden on those in work to support the welfare state could become unsustainable.

The problem is that public services have been planned on the assumption of rapid economic growth. Cuts imposed by governments since the mid-1970s have been seen as essentially short-term expedients. There has been little or no consideration of what should happen to the welfare state if the economy stagnates indefinitely.

Nowhere is this better illustrated than in the case of pensions. Barbara Castle's ambitious plan enacted in 1975 provides for earnings-related, inflation-proofed (or nearly) pensions for all. The White Paper introducing the scheme stated optimistically: 'The (new) scheme will lead to a gradual increase in transfer of income and therefore of claims on resources from the economically active sector of the community to those who have retired. . . . (It) will mean that take-home pay of employees will be restricted and prices increased compared with what would otherwise have been the case. . . . But the full costs . . . will be far outweighed by the improvement in living standards generally resulting from economic growth.'

Independent estimates of the cost of the Castle scheme plus some very modest moves towards lower retirement ages and so on suggest that by the first decade of the next century the cost of state pension provision could double in real terms, implying a rise in the average tax burden on those in work from 25 per cent in 1980-81 to 40 per cent. This is equivalent to a transfer of income from workers to pensioners of under 0.4 per cent each year – which might not meet with great resistance if real incomes are growing at 2 to 3 per cent a year but could prove intolerable if growth were much less than this. Since the pensions White Paper was written, national output has risen on average by less than 1 per cent a year.

Pension Payments as % of Total Personal Income

	Occupational pensions	*State pensions*	*Total*
1955	1¼	2¾	4
1975	3	4¾	7¾
1980	4	5	9
2000	6½	7	13½
2030	*	*	17

*not available
Source: 'Occupational pension schemes – economic background and issues' by Professor Harold Rose in *The Economics of Pension Arrangements*, Bank of England Panel of Academic Consultants, Panel Paper 20, March 1983

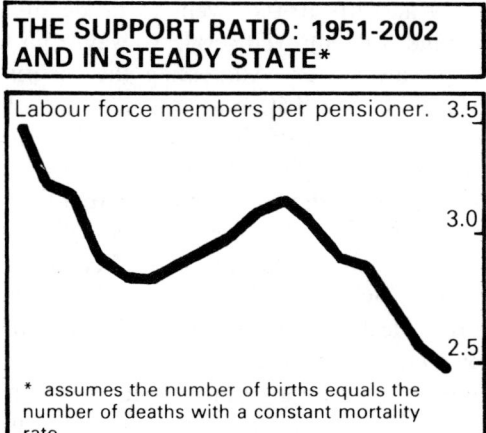

Source: J. Ermisch, 'Paying the piper: demographic changes and pension contributions', *Policy Studies*, no. 1, 1981. London: Policy Studies Institute.

Even where no significant improvements are planned, the cost of public services seems set to rocket. A confidential paper recently submitted to the Cabinet by an inter-departmental group of officials suggested that health spending could rise in real terms by 25 to 35 per cent during the 1980s, mainly because of population changes, while social security spending could increase by 20 to 25 per cent, in large part the consequence of continuing high unemployment.

With a growth rate of around 2.5 per cent a year, close to 'the best we can expect', public spending would absorb roughly the same proportion – 37 per cent instead of 38 per cent – of national output in 1990 as it did in 1979-80. With slow growth – 0.5 to 0.75 per cent a year – the proportion could rise to 44 per cent. These figures exclude interest on government debt.

But the higher growth scenario makes virtually no concession to public demand for better services as national wealth increases. There is plenty of evidence from abroad to show that richer societies choose to spend a higher proportion of their incomes on health care, education and social services. The pressure will always be there for spending on public services to outstrip the growth in economic output, while the gains of prosperity are not willingly relinquished when times are harder.

Sir Geoffrey and Mr Brittan want to tackle this problem by diverting demand for improved services away from the state and towards the private sector. Addressing the Institute for Fiscal Studies in May 1982, Mr Brittan argued in favour of maintaining an absolute basic level of public services rather than a relative level as a proportion of national output. People had inflated expectations of what the state could provide in straitened economic circumstances. 'The real question', he suggested, 'is how much the state can afford to provide, free, and still leave the individual citizen with the incentive and ability on top of that . . . to provide for his own old age, his own health and his own children's education, directly.'

It is an interesting paradox that people are often prepared to spend more out of their own pockets than they grudge the state in taxes to pay for the services they want. But even granted this paradox the Conservative solution has three critical flaws.

First, simply shifting the financial burden of health, pensions and education from taxes to take-home pay does not leave people better-off on balance. In practice it could leave them worse-off if private provision is dearer, as it often is.

Second, such a shift implies that services will be allocated, not on the basis of need – the very *raison d'être* of the welfare state – but on the basis of ability to pay. In other words, poor people will get a second-class service – or none at all. Arguing that the shift would apply only to services above a basic minimum merely begs the question of what the minimum is. If it is set low the full force of the criticism applies. If it is set high the savings on public spending will be trivial.

Third, the very existence of a private sector can detract from the state service, tempting away skilled people with higher salaries and better working conditions and, with schools, removing bright, well-motivated children with parents who can afford to pay to the detriment of those remaining behind.

If two-tier public services are no solution, however, another must be found. There is a limit to how much in taxes working people are prepared to pay and the squeeze on their living standards they will tolerate. The danger is that if public services are not carefully planned and expectations deflated to allow for the possibility that economic growth will not automatically provide, the cost time bomb may explode and the welfare state with it.

In the autumn of 1982 the Cabinet was presented with a paper from the Central Policy Review Staff (the government's official Think Tank, abolished shortly after the 1983 general election). This suggested that if the government wished to stop public spending rising under conditions of slow growth it would need to prune the welfare state dramatically. Options canvassed included moving from a tax-financed to an insurance-based health care system, replacing student grants with loans, and cutting the link between social security benefits and inflation.

The Cabinet, flabbergasted, refused even to discuss the CPRS paper at the time. Its subsequent leak caused a political storm, which led to the report being hurriedly shelved. No decisions were ever taken on it, but the controversy persisted throughout the 1983 general election campaign, with the opposition parties accusing the government of concealing a 'hidden manifesto' to dismantle the welfare state.

4 Moving to a balanced budget?

Published February 23 1983

The government can pump demand into the economy or withdraw demand from it by altering its own budget balance. If it boosts spending or cuts taxes, the budget deficit widens and policy is expansionary. If it reduces spending or puts up taxes, the budget deficit narrows and policy is contractionary.

Even if the government makes no tax or spending changes, however, the actual budget balance will vary at different stages of the economic cycle. When the economy is in recession and unemployment is rising, the budget deficit automatically increases as the government spends more on social benefits and gets back less in taxes. This helps to stimulate the economy and put it back on a path to recovery. When output is rising and unemployment falling the reverse happens.

22 *Economic Overview*

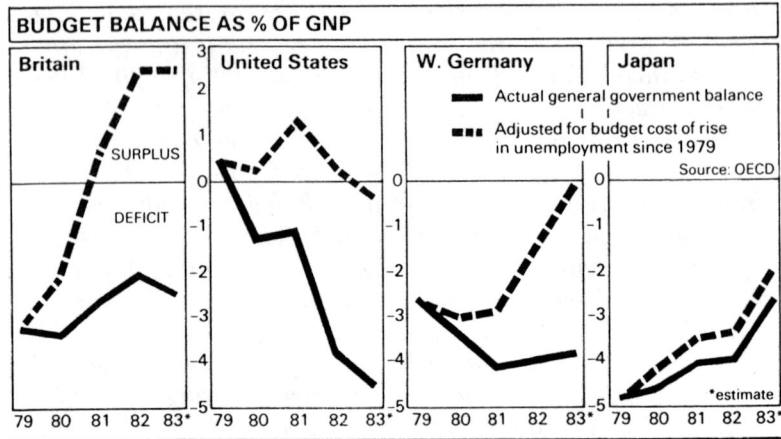

These 'built-in stabilisers' complicate assessment of fiscal policy. Many economists believe a better guide to fiscal stance is the 'high employment' or 'cyclically adjusted' budget balance – what the deficit would be if the economy were running at full capacity. This is sometimes termed the **structural**, as opposed to the **cyclical**, budget deficit.

A rising government deficit during recession is thus not necessarily expansionary if it simply reflects the impact of higher unemployment.

Adjusted for recession, Britain's budget deficit disappears. If the economy returned to more prosperous days the government would be in substantial structural surplus. In other words, its fiscal policy has been highly contractionary.

There are other ways of looking at the budget balance. Inflation erodes the real value of debt denominated in cash terms. This benefits the government as a massive debtor to the public. It means that all or part of the interest paid on its debt is just compensation to the lenders for the drop in the value of their assets. It is also possible to argue that public investment ought to be excluded from any balanced budget requirement because it is sensible to finance it through borrowing. This spreads the cost more fairly between generations who benefit from it.

The present government has never admitted having an independent fiscal policy. It has a fiscal strategy – to bring down public borrowing steadily as a proportion of national output. But the official line is that this is necessary to help curb money growth – the government's primary target – without forcing up interest rates. It is not an end in itself.

The fact that it has been a good deal more successful in achieving lower public borrowing than it has lower money growth or interest rates has not been allowed to affect the government's argument. Logically there need be no end to the process. Public borrowing could go on being reduced, if necessary repaying debt, until monetary expansion was thought to be compatible with ministers' ultimate inflation objectives. After all, Mrs Thatcher has made it clear that her long-term goal is zero inflation.

Once this is achieved, however, what should the government's budget policy be? Ministers have decisively rejected the pre-1979 pragmatism under which chancellors started with the deficit or surplus thrown up by current policies, then added or subtracted to boost or restrain demand. This was both ineffective and inflationary, ministers believe, leading under the inevitable political pressures simply to ever-higher deficits in the long run.

The most obvious alternative – and the only systematic alternative so far proposed – is for the government to aim for a balanced budget, matching state expenditures and revenues in the classic Victorian way. This would mean no regular public borrowing and no contribution from the state sector to money growth.

Professor Alan Walters, who as the Prime Minister's personal economic adviser is very much on the inside track of radical Conservative Party thinking, certainly supports such an objective. What is more, he believes the government is already well on the way towards balancing its books, taking the present economic cycle as a whole.

Mere balance, however, would imply little hope of reducing unemployment significantly, even when the economy picks up. It is a measure of how tight the government's fiscal stance has become that if the number of jobless were back at 1979 levels – less than 1.5 million – rather than today's 3 million plus the government would be running a huge budget surplus. Mr Gavyn Davies of the stockbroking firm, Simon and Coates, has calculated that government borrowing of an estimated £7,500m in 1982-83[1] would be transformed into a £4,700 m surplus at 1979

1 Public borrowing turned out at £9,200m in 1982-83.

24 Economic Overview

jobless levels. Unemployment in total cost the government nearly £14,000m in lost revenues and higher social security payouts in 1982-83, the Institute for Fiscal Studies estimates, close to double its likely borrowing for the year.

But the size of the cyclical adjustment to nominal public borrowing depends on what the people advocating it think unemployment 'ought' to be, a subject on which there is no identifiable consensus. If unemployment is expected to stick at around present levels, as most forecasters predict, the cyclically adjusted high employment budget balance is not much use to a government wanting to balance its books in practice within a reasonably short timespan. To adopt such a target would also imply that the government had an employment objective and an obligation to meet it, which the present administration rejects absolutely.

Ministers do accept that government borrowing should normally be allowed to rise in recession, as Mr Nigel Lawson, then Financial Secretary to the Treasury, made clear in a notable speech in Zurich early in 1981. But in practice ministers put their monetary and inflation objectives first. Instead, recession simply slowed progress to a lower deficit. The original medium-term financial strategy published in the 1980 Budget envisaged slashing the public sector borrowing requirement from 5 per cent of national output in 1979-80 to 1.5 per cent in 1982-83. This compares with the 1982 Budget forecast of 3.5 per cent.[1]

It is occasionally argued that budget deficits should be adjusted for inflation, to take account of the fact that much of the government's interest payments simply offsets the falling real value of its debt. As a huge net debtor the government benefits from inflation. Stockbrokers Laing and Cruickshank believe that this inflation gain has averaged £12,500m a year since 1979-80, more than wiping out total public borrowing over the three years. In the 1982-83 financial year the inflation-adjusted government financial balance was an estimated £1,000m in surplus.

The trouble with this concept is that it is not operationally helpful. The 'real' PSBR has been in surplus in almost every year since the war. Trying to keep it constant would mean raising the nominal amount of borrowing whenever inflation rose – for instance because of higher commodity prices, outside government influence. This would tend to accommodate the inflation instead

1 See table on p. 6.

of dampening it down as the government would want to do.

Finally, people argue that the government should aim for balance only on current account, with capital investment financed through borrowing. If capital spending is included in the requirement for budget balance, the present generation of taxpayers is penalised by having to pay the whole cost of investments which will benefit future generations.

Support for borrowing to finance capital spending comes from Keynesians and monetarists alike. A well-known American monetarist, Mr Thomas Sargent from the University of Minnesota, pointed out in a 1981 paper that 'the principles of classical economic theory condone government deficits on capital account. . . . In short, so far as capital account deficits are concerned, there is a sense in which a government is like a firm, it being wise to borrow in order to finance worthwhile long-lived projects with taxes and other user charges whose stream over time matches the time-profile of benefits.'

For the last three years, however, capital spending by the public sector has substantially exceeded borrowing, in 1982-83 by a margin of perhaps £3,500m. This is despite a sharp drop in public investment in real, inflation-adjusted terms.[1] Investment still exceeds borrowing even if the state industry sector is split off. In 1982-83, for instance, borrowing by central and local government together on their own account was planned to total £6,000m compared with budgeted capital spending of £7,000m.

Ministers nevertheless find little favour in arguments that investment should be treated differently, insisting that whatever public borrowing is for it still has to be financed in the market without 'unacceptable consequences' for the money supply, the exchange rate, interest rates and inflation.

The government does not have an explicit balanced budget objective. But, whether deliberately or not, it has clearly eliminated Britain's structural deficit. All the adjustments – for the economic cycle, for inflation, for capital spending – produce a budget surplus. The government could well decide to aim for a zero nominal budget balance as an adjunct to monetary policy, perhaps with some deviation either side to allow for changes in economic activity. But this is not at all the same thing as the neutral fiscal stance which the notion of a balanced budget implies.

5 Tax cuts only for some

Published March 7 1983

'We need to strengthen incentives, by allowing people to keep more of what they earn, so that hard work, talent and ability are properly rewarded,' argued Sir Geoffrey Howe in his first Budget in June 1979. Stressing the need to cut income tax at all levels, he said the government's long-term aim was to cut the basic rate of tax to no more than 25 per cent.

All this makes wistful reading today. Sir Geoffrey approaches his fifth and possibly last Budget in the knowledge that under his Chancellorship the burden of personal taxes has risen steeply for all except the highest income earners. It is no wonder, then, that the Prime Minister, backed by the majority of her Cabinet, is eager to see personal taxes cut in the 1983 Budget.

Alas, Sir Geoffrey's supposed Budget largesse – of the order of £2,000m – goes nowhere near what is needed to compensate for the rise in the tax burden over which he has unwillingly presided. To restore taxes paid by households (income tax, national insurance contributions and spending taxes such as VAT and excise duties) to their 1978-79 levels in real terms would cost the Exchequer a staggering £9,000m in 1983-84 – equivalent to cutting the basic rate of income tax by 9p in the pound.

Things went wrong for two main reasons: deteriorating state finances and recession. The government failed to get a firm grip on public spending early on, with the result that spending in 1982-83 is running some £6,600m higher than planned four years ago. Without the more rapid than expected drop in inflation over the past 12 months the overspend would have topped £8,000m. At the same time, ministers were determined to cut government borrowing as part of their battle against inflation. So taxes had to go up not just to pay for the extra spending but for reducing state borrowing as well.

The severe recession – itself exacerbated by tough government policies to fight inflation – has also led to the loss of more than two million jobs. Higher unemployment adds to public spending because more social security benefits have to be paid out. And the necessary taxes have to be shared out among fewer and fewer people still in work. In 1978-79, taxes in total represented 34 per cent of national output. In 1982, the latest available year, the proportion had jumped to an all-time high of 40 per cent. The real tax burden rose while national output fell.

Sir Geoffrey's first Budget instituted a big shift from taxes on income to taxes on spending, in pursuit of improved incentives. He cut the top rates of income tax, lowered the basic rate from 33p to 30p in the pound and raised thresholds by twice the amount needed to compensate for inflation. At the same time he doubled VAT from 8 per cent (with a 12.5 per cent luxury rate) to 15 per cent. The rise in VAT – which covers about half of all household spending – almost exactly offset the gains from lower income tax for most people. The affluent did best – the cuts in income tax far outweighed the extra VAT. The poor fared worst. They paid relatively little income tax – but could not escape VAT.

Since 1979, taxes on spending have risen broadly in line with inflation. But taxes on income have risen steeply. In 1980, the Chancellor indexed the thresholds to inflation but abolished the 25 per cent reduced rate band for low incomes. He then stunned supporters and opponents alike in 1981 by refusing to raise personal tax allowances at all despite 15 per cent inflation over the previous year. This loss has not been made good. In 1982 Sir Geoffrey increased allowances by only 2 per cent more than the rise in prices.

The vast majority of earners now pay more of their incomes in income tax than in 1978-79. And all employees are paying extra in national insurance contributions. These have risen steadily from 6.5 per cent in 1979 to 8.75 per cent today (and are due to go up to 9 per cent in April 1983). Taking income tax and national insurance contributions together, only those earning £30,000 a year or more – three and a half times the average – are paying less tax in real terms than in 1978-79. As a proportion of incomes, only those earning over £23,000 – two and a half times the average – are paying less tax.

So much for the average tax burden. But for incentives it is the marginal rate of tax – the tax on each extra pound of income – that is most relevant. Some people argue that there is no difference between direct (income) taxes and indirect (spending) taxes where incentives are concerned. It is the total tax on each extra pound of income that matters, however it is levied. On this basis, incentives for most people have weakened. But even if we accept the government's view that only direct taxes (which

28 *Economic Overview*

include national insurance contributions) matter for incentives, the picture is little improved. For most people the marginal rate of tax has remained broadly unchanged. For the poor the fall in the value of the tax threshold has made incentives worse.

After the much-vaunted 1979 switch from direct to indirect taxes the proportions have been gradually reasserting themselves. In 1978-79 direct taxes accounted for 48.5 per cent of revenues, indirect taxes 51.5 per cent. The next year those proportions became 45.5 and 54.5 per cent respectively. In 1982-83, direct taxes accounted for 48 per cent of the total, while indirect taxes had fallen back to 52 per cent.

To restore personal tax allowances to their same real level as in 1978-79, adjusted for inflation, would involve raising them by 8.5 per cent in the 1983 Budget, 3 per cent more than indexation alone. But because earnings have risen faster than prices, simply restoring the value of the threshold in real terms would still mean an increase in income tax as a proportion of income and more people paying tax than before.

To restore personal allowances to the same proportion of average earnings as in 1978-79 would mean raising them by 10 per cent more than inflation in the 1983 Budget. This would take about 850,000 people out of the tax net. This, many commentators assume, is what the Chancellor and the Prime Minister intend to do. It would enable them to claim, at the very least, that income tax had not risen over their period of office. But that is all. National insurance and VAT will still be higher than before. As far as the great majority of people in Britain are concerned, taxes have gone up. This is not what they were promised.

In the 1983 Budget, his last, Sir Geoffrey Howe raised personal tax allowances by 14 per cent – some 8.5 per cent more than the rise in prices in 1982 – and indexed excise duties. The Budget stimulus was equivalent to £2,200m in a full year.

The rise in tax thresholds was enough to restore them to the same level in real terms as in 1978-79, but not enough to restore them to the same proportion of earnings. Though most families paid a slightly smaller share of their earnings in income tax alone in 1983-84 than in 1978-79, because of the 1979 cut of 3p in the basic rate, higher national insurance contributions ensured that all but the rich faced a heavier tax burden.

6 Giving state industries room to breathe

Published February 4 1981

The reduction of state industry calls on the Exchequer for loans and grants, by eliminating losses and boosting the proportion of their investment financed internally, has been a key component of the government's attempts to restrain overall public borrowing. Its first public spending white paper in 1980 envisaged a huge turnround in industry finances from a borrowing requirement of £2,300m (at 1979 survey prices) in 1979-80 to a net repayment to the Exchequer of £400m in 1983-84.

The government hoped that tight constraints on the funds

available to state industries would force them to improve efficiency and keep pay settlements down, rather than sacrifice services or investment. In practice, however, investment plans were hit while industries in a strong market position, such as gas and electricity, were able to put up prices to generate more revenue.

This strengthened ministers' determination to push ahead with the privatisation of profitable or potentially profitable state enterprises. It was not just a way of shuffling off their financing needs to the private sector. It fulfilled the government's broader objective of rolling back the frontiers of the state's involvement in the economy. And it supported its 'supply-side' philosophy that in private hands the disciplines of the market place would oblige the industries to become more efficient and dynamic, with economic benefits to the nation as a whole.

But recession held up the government's ambitious plans. Ministers were forced to give way time and again to industry demands for more cash, as trading conditions worsened. And the dismal financial performance of industries earmarked for sale put back the timetable for privatisation.

Direct access to financial institutions is just one of the reforms being urged on ministers and officials by nationalised industry chiefs, alarmed by the damaging constraints on their investment imposed by strict borrowing limits.

At the root of the problem is the government's use of external financing limits (EFLs) as a means of controlling the public sector borrowing requirement. These limit the sums which state industries can raise through borrowing, grants and subsidies, to supplement internally generated revenue. EFLs, which represent the contribution of nationalised industries to the PSBR, have become increasingly stringent over the past couple of years, as the government has attempted to tighten the screw on public spending. Even the higher external financing limits for 1981-82 announced in November 1980 only partially compensate for the impact of the recession on revenues and require the industries to make cuts in planned spending totalling more than £1,000m.

Denied the opportunity to borrow all they need to carry out their investment programmes, the industries have had little choice but to prune them back, attempt to generate more cash by

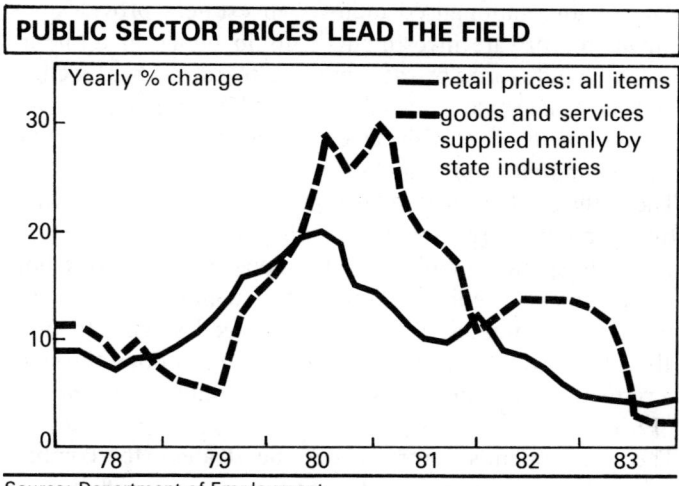

Source: Department of Employment

increasing prices or scale down services or production. Investment by nationalised industries has been falling since 1976 while the price index for consumer goods and services supplied by them has been rising consistently faster than prices in general – by 30 per cent in 1980 which was twice the average inflation rate.

The nationalised industry chairmen believe that government policy is fundamentally misguided. Productive investment which can be shown to bring economic benefits to the industry and to the nation should be judged on its merits, they argue. A project providing a good rate of return does not become less desirable because it is undertaken by a public corporation rather than a private company. Counting nationalised industry borrowings within the public sector is merely an accounting convention, not a representation of real economic differences. The industries do not accept that their investment should be constrained to help fulfil global public spending targets, in which no distinction is made between social spending (a charge on economic resources) and productive investment (an addition to those resources).[1]

Sir Derek Ezra, the present chairman of the Nationalised Industries' Chairmen's Group, has forcefully argued that, far from pre-empting resources which would otherwise go to the

---

1 See argument for financing investment through borrowing in 'Moving to a balanced budget?', p. 21.

private sector, nationalised industry investment provides a vital stimulant for private investment. Cuts in public investment, on the other hand, force private industry to retrench as well. Less Coal Board investment means less need for mining machinery. Less investment by British Telecom means fewer opportunities for telecommunications suppliers.

The official Treasury line remains that all borrowing by statutory public corporations for whatever purpose must come within state spending controls. The industries effectively borrow on government credit and so offer comparatively risk-free investment indistinguishable from gilt-edged stock. (In practice all their borrowing from UK capital markets is done through the government – but even if it were not, it would still count against the PSBR.)

The government's central economic strategy for combatting inflation through control of the money supply and hence the PSBR must take precedence over individual investment decisions.[1] According to this view, the only way in which investment can legitimately be taken out of public sector control is for the industry itself, in whole or in part, to become a private concern – a course which in any case commends itself to a government with an ideological (if not always practical) commitment to reducing state involvement in industry.

The government intends to make British Aerospace (with a prospectus out at the end of this week), British Airways, the National Freight Company and the British Transport Docks Board[2] into private companies, with all or part of their share capital sold off to private investors when market conditions permit. As private companies, they will then be able to borrow direct from private capital markets, outside the PSBR and free of government controls.

British Rail and British Telecom are to be allowed to form subsidiaries involving private capital (which could become private companies at a later date – in BR's case its cross-channel ferry, hovercraft, hotel and certain property operations).

The industries are also trying to identify specific investment projects which could attract private capital. British Rail is

1 In practice, the amount of investment discouraged by borrowing curbs may have amounted to no more than £500m, according to a 1981 report from the Treasury Select Committee of MPs, though this figure did not include major projects still under discussion such as main-line electrification.
2 Now Associated British Ports.

exploring ways of financing main-line electrification privately, with BR leasing back the equipment from the private sector. British Gas will be partners in a new private company to build the North Sea gas gathering pipeline. The Channel Tunnel, the government hopes, will be entirely financed by the private sector.

Though in principle privatisation seems straightforward, its definition in practice is not so simple. It is certainly not a question of who owns the company. The government owns 95 per cent of British Leyland – but it counts as a private company, and its private borrowings (as opposed to government assistance) do not figure in the PSBR. The British National Oil Corporation, on the other hand, which is only 51 per cent government-owned, is a nationalised industry and all its borrowings, from whatever source, count towards the PSBR. The deciding factors, according to the Treasury, are: who has control? who bears the risk? If the government decides not to make use of its shareholding, however large, to control a company then control passes to the private owners and the borrowings of that company are excluded from the PSBR. In addition, the government must refuse to guarantee the enterprise against loss. Investors then face commercial risks which ensures that the borrowings will not compete with sales of government debt.

But these distinctions may not be clearly apparent in practice. However hard the government protests that it does not intend to use its shareholding in British Aerospace to control the company, nor to guarantee the company against loss, are investors really going to believe that British Aerospace, with its important defence contracts, will be allowed to go bust? At what level (and concentration) of private shareholding will British Rail or British Telecom be told to relinquish control over their subsidiaries and to whom – 30 per cent (in the hands of one owner), 50 per cent (owned by many)? And will these subsidiaries be genuinely less credit-worthy than their parents? If not, their borrowings will still fall within the PSBR (if publicly controlled) or compete with gilts (if privately controlled). Also, how can the government avoid implicit guarantees on private investment connected with nationalised industries? How can the Channel Tunnel or railway electrification bear normal commercial risks when government-backed British Rail will be the monopoly user?

These are problems the government is currently wrestling with. Unless it comes up with a clear distinction, especially in terms of risk, between investment in companies it transfers to the private sector and in corporations remaining in the public sector, the difference between the two will be no more than an accounting sleight of hand. In that case, privatisation is unlikely to release any extra real resources for investment that could not have been achieved through relaxation of EFLs and access by the nationalised industries to private capital markets, as they have urged.

By the end of 1983, plans to introduce private capital into state industry operations had made little progress, though a number of schemes, including the upgrading of British Rail's Victoria-Gatwick link, were under discussion. Meanwhile, investment by nationalised enterprises scarcely kept pace with capital consumption. In 1982, net investment was actually negative.

In 1983-84, the industries had external financing needs of £2,625m, compared with the net repayment to Exchequer coffers envisaged in 1980. Present government plans foresee some reduction in future years to £1,803m in 1985-86, a more modest objective than before.

But the government was able to press ahead with its privatisation programme. By the time of the 1983 election, British Aerospace, Cable and Wireless, the National Freight Company, Amersham International, Associated British Ports and the British National Oil Corporation had all been sold into the private sector. So had some British Rail hotels. On the list for the government's second term were British Telecom, the oil interests of British Gas, other British Rail subsidiaries, British Airways, the British Airports Authority, the National Bus Company, the Royal Ordnance Factories and profitable subsidiaries of BL, such as Jaguar. These are expected to raise £2,000m a year between 1983 and 1988.

Asset sales help the government to balance its books. They count as reducing public spending (though they could just as well be thought of as another way of financing government borrowing as an alternative to sales of gilts). But assets can only be sold once, leaving ministers open to charges that they are 'selling the furniture to pay the housekeeping.'

II Economic Overview: The Issues of Mrs Thatcher's Second Term

Introduction

Mrs Thatcher always said she needed a second term to demonstrate the rightness of her economic policies. Now she has that second term and must deliver the electoral goodies on cue. She will not be given a third mandate on trust.

In the 1983 election year, recovery had clearly begun but it remained patchy and fragile. Consumer industries were doing well (and foreign consumer industries even better) from the buying spree sparked off by relaxation of credit controls in the summer of 1982, lower mortgage rates, and rising real incomes for those in work. Other industries were still feeling the pinch.

The upswing, which officially 'began' in spring 1981 when national output touched its nadir, was the slowest in Britain's post-war history. Indeed, until 1983 it could scarcely be called a recovery since output growth remained well below the likely expansion of productive potential, widening the 'output gap' and increasing spare capacity in the economy. By then, however, the government was confidently claiming that the economic turnabout vindicated monetarist economic policies. It showed that Keynesian-style reflation was unnecessary to bring about renewed growth. Instead lower inflation and interest rates had stimulated consumer spending, largely by reducing the proportion of income saved. Lower inflation meant people did not need to put by so much to maintain the real value of their assets (the so-called 'wealth effect'). Lower interest rates – helped by abolition of HP controls – made credit cheaper. In time, the Treasury argued, improved competitiveness – through lower pay deals and enhanced productivity – would boost exports while increased

35

company profitability – through moderation of their costs – would lead to greater investment and stockbuilding.

Keynesians prefer to point to the government's looser fiscal and monetary stance in 1982-83 and the drop in the exchange rate as the chief cause of the pickup in activity. The government did not reduce public spending plans or monetary targets when inflation fell faster than expected, so permitting a stronger real increase in home demand, while the decline in sterling brightened the outlook for exports. Keynesians had to acknowledge, however, that the strength of the wealth effect, augmented by people's willingness to borrow an ever-higher proportion of their incomes, had been greater than they predicted.

Ministers are hopeful that investment and exports will take over from consumer spending as the driving force behind the upswing in 1984 and beyond. But many outside forecasters are sceptical whether their revival will be sufficiently robust to compensate for the tailing off of the consumer boom. The savings ratio, which halved between 1980 and 1983, is expected to stabilise at around its present level of 8 per cent as inflation sticks around present levels of 5 per cent or so and families hesitate to go deeper into debt.

The next couple of years will be the test of the government's contention that low inflation and sustained growth can go hand in hand. A lot of economists still believe that there is a long-run trade-off between inflation and unemployment. You can have more growth but only at the cost of more inflation. But the government and monetarist economists disagree.

The Chancellor, Mr Nigel Lawson, has claimed that experience since the recovery began in 1981 backs the government's case. Inflation has halved since that time, despite a pick-up in economic growth. However, the economy only started to expand at a moderate pace late in 1982. The impact on unemployment was not felt until the second half of 1983. So the true test will come in 1984 and 1985 if the recovery is sustained.

Mrs Thatcher needs to be able to deliver three election gifts by summer 1988 at the latest: continuing low (but not necessarily much lower) inflation, declining unemployment and tax cuts. Neither of the last two can be achieved without economic growth. So ministers will be under pressure to give growth a greater priority and the further reduction of inflation a lesser one. This shift of emphasis is likely to be reinforced by two constraining influences on the government's room to manoeuvre. North Sea oil revenues, which obviated the need for an even bigger increase in personal taxes in Mrs Thatcher's first term, may be falling by 1988. And public spending is expected to prove a difficult animal to control, especially if high unemployment continues to push up the social security budget.

The section starts with 'The June 1983 election: the most uncertain choice', which summarises the economic policies pursued in the government's first term of office and their outcome, and compares the aspirations of the three major parties. 'This time oil must be made to pay' looks at what has happened to North Sea oil revenues and the problems confronting the government as these stabilise and then decline in the second half of the decade. The reliance of government hopes for the success of its economic policies on achieving reasonable growth over the next few years is the theme of 'Proving the pain was worthwhile', and this is followed by a discussion of the difficulties it faces in curbing public spending in 'Facing up to the public spending Leviathan'. The section ends with 'The black hole in the economy', a review of research on the size of the hidden economy.

1 The June 1983 election: the most uncertain choice

Published May 26 1983

The general election, won by the Conservatives with a thumping Parliamentary majority, was held on Thursday June 9 1983

Rarely can the electorate have been presented with so uncertain a choice as they now face between the competing economic promises of the parties.

On the one hand, Mrs Margaret Thatcher is asking for a vote of confidence in tough anti-inflation policies which she claims have 'laid the foundations for a dynamic and prosperous future' but which so far have accompanied the devastation of British industry and soaring unemployment.

On the other hand, Mr Michael Foot is promising the creation of 2.5 million jobs in five years – a feat surpassed only by postwar demobilisation – through a huge reflation programme, the very thought of which has made the City's hair stand on end. Yet without the confidence of financial markets, as President Mitterrand of France has found to his cost, the best-laid plans of socialist governments may come to grief.

Between the two lie the modest expansion plans of the untried, largely inexperienced Alliance, risking less, but for lower stakes than the others, with their counter-inflation hopes resting largely on a novel form of permanent statutory incomes policy.

Mrs Thatcher has the disadvantage of having to ask for a judgement on her record when, as she has repeatedly made clear, her economic experiment is only half-way through. She came to office dedicated to shaking up the traditional post-war economic consensus. The reduction of inflation replaced commitment to full employment as the prime objective of policy. Management of demand in the economy gave way to controlling the money supply as the principal tool. Responsibility for economic growth was shifted from the government's shoulders to those of management and workers, expected to respond to a new framework of incentives in which big tax cuts would play a central role.

In its prime objective, the government can claim considerable success. Inflation, more than 10 per cent and rising when Mrs Thatcher assumed power in May 1979, is now 4 per cent, putting Britain among the low inflation countries of the world for the first time in many years. But this has not been brought about by controlling the money supply, which overshot its targets in three of the four years. Instead, partly deliberately and partly unintentionally, the government engineered an old-fashioned recession. It cut the budget deficit at a time when rising unemployment would normally push it up, tightening fiscal policy more severely than any other industrial country. And it allowed high interest rates and the rapid build-up of North Sea oil production to drive the international value of the pound to lethally uncompetitive levels.

This helped inflation by cheapening imports. But it pushed a large part of British industry into bankruptcy. Since June 1979, when the downturn began, industrial production has slumped by nearly 9 per cent and manufacturing output by almost 16 per cent, with the loss of a quarter of the workforce. In the first quarter of 1983, Britain sustained a deficit on manufactured trade for the first time since the Industrial Revolution 200 years ago. Most damningly, unemployment has trebled from 1.2 million, or 5 per cent of the workforce, at the time of the 1979 election to over 3 million – 13 per cent – today. The government has also come unstuck with its tax cut hopes. Unable to fulfill promises to slash public spending – not least because of the rising cost of unemployment – but determined to reduce state borrowing, the government has raised taxes by the equivalent of 7p in the pound.

Now, in the midst of the worst recession for 50 years, the Conservatives are asking for another go. 'In the next Parliament', the manifesto says, 'we shall endeavour to bring inflation lower still. Our ultimate goal should be for a society with stable prices.' The questions voters must ask themselves are these: Will progress to lower inflation through the firm money and fiscal policies that are promised stimulate or hinder recovery? Will pay and price moderation, induced by fears of redundancy and closure, persist once demand revives and job prospects improve? Has the recession produced a permanent shift in attitudes and working practices capable of delivering a better growth performance than Britain has had in the past?

Mrs Thatcher has no doubts. Independent observers, and some within her own party, are more sceptical. The immediate outlook is not promising, with most forecasters including the Treasury expecting slow growth, higher unemployment and little further reduction in inflation over the next twelve to eighteen months. But even in the longer run, simulations of the Tory economic programme suggest that determined efforts to push down inflation to much lower levels would produce continued sluggish growth and an alarming climb in the number of jobless towards four million.

Labour's plans, however, also fare badly when run through models of the economy. The ambitious jobs target simply looks unattainable on the policies proposed. And all the simulations, including that by the Labour Party itself, show that without restraint on incomes the economy quickly runs aground on the rocks of swiftly accelerating inflation and an unsustainable balance of payments deficit. Labour's answer – the vaguely worded plan for a national economic assessment between

THE ECONOMY UNDER MRS THATCHER

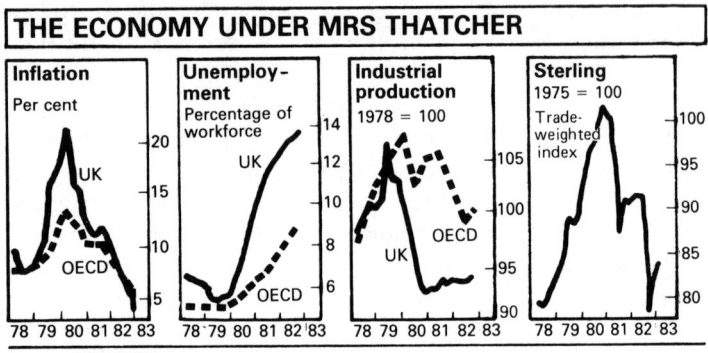

Source: CSO, OECD

Inflation has more than halved from 10.3 per cent in May 1979 to 4 per cent in May 1983 after soaring to a peak of 22 per cent in the spring of 1980.

Unemployment in Britain has risen one and a half times as fast as the industrial country average, trebling from 1.2 million (5 per cent of the workforce) in May 1979 to 3 million (13 per cent) four years later.

Britain has suffered the most severe recession in the West, with industrial production in spring 1983 down 9 per cent on its 1979 peak and manufacturing output down 16 per cent.

The pound soared by 20 per cent between 1979 and early 1981 before dropping back to previous levels. But industry's competitiveness abroad, eroded by high pay deals in the first year, was still 20 per cent worse in spring 1983 than four years earlier.

---

government and unions – has carried little conviction.

The Alliance plans to create one million jobs within two years, largely through special job measures, and is committed to a fully-fledged incomes policy to contain inflation – though past experience suggests that an incomes policy with teeth is hard to sustain for long. Feeding Alliance policies through the economic models gives, predictably, a 'middle way' – more growth and jobs than Conservative policies (and more inflation) but less than a successful Labour programme.

The voters' choice is thus less simple than it seems. It is not merely between inflation and unemployment as the prime imperatives of the next government. It is also between the credibility of the packages on offer in a harsh and uncertain world.

2 This time oil must be made to pay

Published June 11 1983

Mrs Thatcher's government has been the first to enjoy the fruits of Britain's North Sea oil wealth. Without the £20,000m of oil revenues flowing into Exchequer coffers over the four years since 1979, money that simply was not there before, she might not today be celebrating her landslide. Her economic programme would almost certainly have been unworkable and its costs insupportable.

If the government had tried to pursue the same tough anti-inflation policies in the absence of oil, according to one recent study by the independent National Institute of Economic and Social Research, the recession would have been twice as deep, unemployment more than a million higher, the balance of payments in huge deficit and income tax would have had to go up to 50p in the pound. Inflation would still have been higher than it is today.

The Prime Minister will not be so blessed this time. Oil revenues are expected to peak within the next year or two, at perhaps £10,000m[1] or so a year, and then to stabilise or decline for the remainder of the decade. Instead of an extra £20,000m from oil Mrs Thatcher can bank on only half that sum or less in *additional* government revenues over the next five years.

This places an important constraint on her room to manœuvre. She cannot afford a deeper recession because the extra oil revenues will not be there to cushion its effects. That means that her passionate personal desire to force inflation down to zero, which many economists believe would lead to continued sluggish growth and mounting unemployment, may have to take second place to policies designed to sustain economic recovery. This is however a matter of tactics rather than strategy. The basic approach to the use of North Sea oil receipts is likely to remain unchanged. By the end of the 1980s, with revenues in decline, what benefits will Britain have to show for its short-lived oil bonanza?[2]

1 Peak of closer to £11,000m now expected in 1986 or thereabouts.
2 Also see 'Missing the target on overseas investment', p. 135.

OIL BOUNTY FROM THE NORTH SEA

Contribution to GNP %

Oil revenues £ billion

Oil revenues as % total government revenue

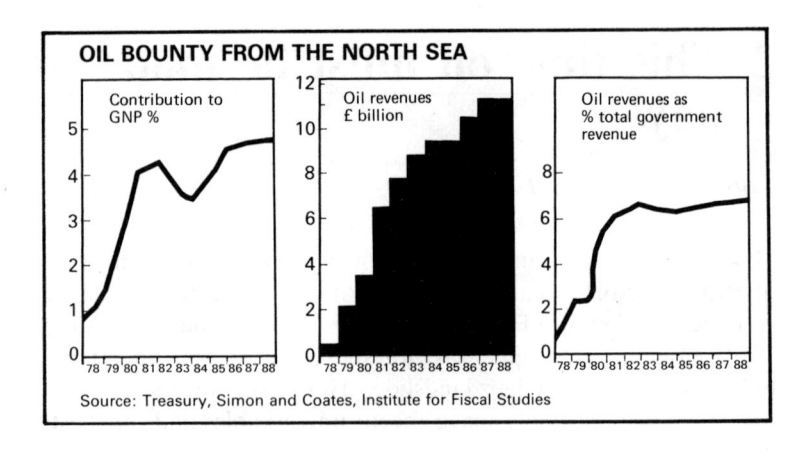

Source: Treasury, Simon and Coates, Institute for Fiscal Studies

Everyone agrees that the principal object of government policy must be to convert the revenues now flowing from oil into investment which will go on providing income after the wells run dry. The Conservative government argued that the best way to stimulate investment was to create the foundations for a healthy economy through reducing inflation. So it harnessed the oil revenues to its tight money and fiscal policies designed to squeeze inflation out of the system. It used them to help cut government borrowing, claiming that this would bring down interest rates and so encourage investment in the private sector. And it allowed sterling, buoyed by oil, to rise to damagingly uncompetitive levels, because this helped the fight against rising prices by making imports cheaper and putting pressure on firms to keep wage costs down. It also boosted the purchasing power of British households and held up consumer spending, which remained broadly constant throughout the worst of the recession.

But the effects on investment were quite the reverse of those intended. Despite lower government borrowing, interest rates remained at historically high levels, especially in inflation-adjusted terms, in the midst of the most severe slump for 50 years, while a beleaguered British industry slashed production, jobs and spending on plant and equipment. Investment funds financed by Britain's oil-enhanced balance of payments surplus flowed abroad, encouraged by the high exchange rate which made foreign assets look cheaper. Between 1979 when exchange controls were abolished and the spring of 1983 about £14,000m went into overseas stocks and shares and a similar sum was invested in the foreign operations of United Kingdom businesses. These assets will be an important source of income when the oil ceases to flow. And to some extent the exodus of funds abroad helped to dampen the increase in the exchange rate and then to bring it down, easing the pressure on industry. But while there is scant evidence to back up Labour's claims that it is harmful, overseas investment does little directly to strengthen Britain's domestic economy, to improve the efficiency of industry or to create jobs for British workers.

There was another way. Oil revenues could have been spent to boost economic activity, for instance through higher public investment and cuts in taxes. The National Institute study, which looked at such a strategy, suggested there would still have been a recession but only a mild one. Instead of a drop in national output of 4 per cent between 1979 and 1982,[1] the reduction would have been only 2 per cent, and unemployment would have been half a million lower. The current account would still have been modestly in surplus. But public borrowing would have been higher and so would inflation, now 4 per cent, by about 2 percentage points.

In effect then, as the study points out, the benefits of oil have been divided between a lower rate of inflation and a considerably higher standard of living for those in work. Without the oil revenues the government could not have cut its borrowing in the face of mounting unemployment, reckoned in 1982 to be costing more than £15,000m in social security benefits and lost taxes, without an even bigger increase in the tax burden.

Whether this amounts to frittering away North Sea riches on financing the dole queues, as the Opposition charges, or the establishment of a sound base for sustained recovery, as the government claims, will be revealed before Mrs Thatcher's second term is out. But Britain's oil opportunity, if it turns out to be wasted, will have come and gone forever.

1 Revised figures now put the drop at only 2.5 per cent.

3 Proving the pain was worthwhile

Published June 15 1983

At first glance the appointment as Chancellor of Mr Nigel Lawson, arch-monetarist and intellectual godfather of the government's medium-term financial plan for curbing inflation, suggests little change in Conservative economic priorities for a second term.

In this case, first impressions are almost certainly misleading. Mr Lawson is likely to prove a far more pragmatic and flexible Chancellor than his predecessor, Sir Geoffrey Howe. This is partly a question of personality: Mr Lawson is a creative and unconventional thinker with a sound grasp of the way the economy works, who is not going to let old orthodoxies stand in the way of fresh ideas. It is also partly a product of circumstances: the world is a different place from the one inhabited by Treasury ministers in 1979. Then, with prices rising at more than 10 per cent a year and accelerating, and memories of the winter of discontent still fresh, inflation seemed the hydra-headed monster barring the way to economic prosperity which had to be subdued at all costs.

The costs have been horrendous – more than two million jobs lost, a fifth of manufacturing industry devastated, national income still some 3 per cent lower than in 1979,[1] but inflation has dropped to a fifteen-year low of 4 per cent and the underlying trend appears to be still slowing. This presents the new government with an entirely different situation. It can no longer reasonably plead that inflation must fall further to permit sustained recovery and more jobs. This time round it has to demonstrate that the previous pain inflicted on the economy in the name of inflation has all been worthwhile.

A fresh drive on inflation through renewed tightening of money and fiscal policies would risk stifling the incipient recovery before it has had time to draw breath. Most outside forecasters expect some cyclical pick-up in inflation as world recovery boosts

1 Revised figures suggest that national income was back to 1979 levels during 1983.

WILL THE ECONOMY CATCH UP?

GDP 1980 = 100

Trend growth of 1.5% per annum

Liverpool University

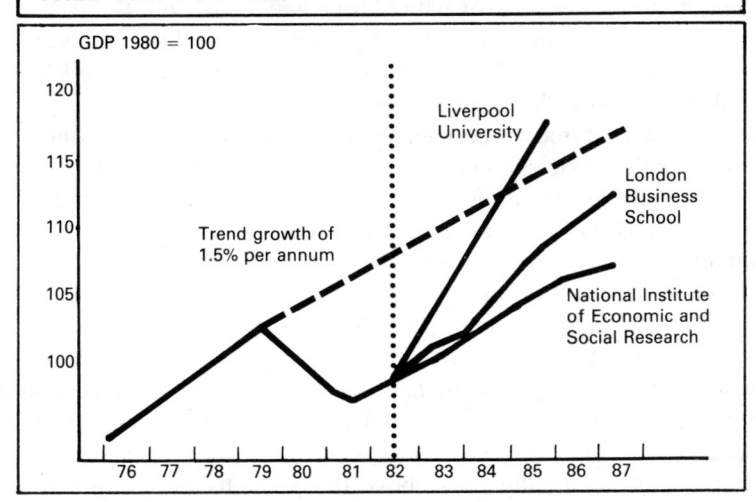

London Business School

National Institute of Economic and Social Research

Note: Liverpool University uses the expenditure measure of gdp.
The other forecasts use the output measure.

commodity prices and companies try to improve profit margins at home. To counteract these pressures and cut the core rate of inflation to very low levels, as Mrs Thatcher would undoubtedly like, could condemn Britain to continued economic stagnation and soaring unemployment, leaving the four million mark well behind.

The human consequences would be appalling; so would the political consequences for Mrs Thatcher. Without growth not only would her tough anti-inflation policies be discredited. Her other objectives – a reduction in public spending and cuts in personal taxes – would be unattainable. Rising unemployment would push up the cost of the social security programme – now more than a quarter of the government's budget. With defence and law and order both programmed to rise in real terms and with health spending planned to keep pace with demographic changes and medical advance, there is precious little left to cut.

These stark facts lay behind Sir Geoffrey Howe's warning to the Cabinet in autumn 1982 that sluggish growth would mean income tax might have to rise to 45p in the pound unless radical measures were taken to reduce public spending. Such an eventuality was only avoided in Mrs Thatcher's first term through the advent of some £20,000m in North Sea oil revenues. They enabled the government to cut its borrowing at relatively small cost in higher personal taxes despite a rise in public spending from 41 to 44 per cent of national income. This time the North Sea will not be so bountiful. Revenues are expected to stabilise in the next couple of years and may be falling by the late 1980s. Unless therefore the economy grows by something like 2.5 per cent a year or more, enough to start bringing unemployment down, both public spending and taxation will have to rise.

Few outside economic forecasters think sustained growth of this order is likely. They expect the recovery to generate fresh inflationary pressures which the government would try to dampen, depressing the economy once again. The majority suggest that national output will finally overtake 1979 levels in 1984 or 1985[1] but that would still leave output well below what it would have been if growth had continued at the pre-recession rate of about 1.5 per cent a year. Unless government policies are successful in inducing the economy to grow faster than that, so that output eventually rises above the previous trend path, the country will be irreversibly the poorer.

The Treasury's own hopes for the economy probably come closest to the projections of 'successful' Conservative policies by the London Business School, from where newly-knighted Sir Terence Burns, the government's chief economic adviser, was plucked in 1979. These show growth close to 2.5 per cent a year between 1983 and 1986, inflation falling gently to around 4 per cent in 1986 after rising in the second half of 1983, and unemployment declining gradually to three million. This would square with Mrs Thatcher's prediction last week on television that she would expect the number of jobless to be down 'certainly by the middle of the next Parliament'.

Officials believe that present financial policies and high unemployment will continue to exert downward pressure on inflation even as growth revives, and that further significant tightening of the economic screw will be unnecessary. Provided that the underlying rate of inflation is in little danger of accelerating, officials will urge the Chancellor to adopt policies designed to encourage growth and the creation of jobs. Price stability, as the Conservative manifesto put it, is an ultimate objective. It is not a proximate one.

This has important consequences for the way Mr Lawson is likely to approach the economy in the coming months. The first

1 Revised figures suggest this point was reached in 1983.

priority will be to keep the fragile upswing intact. The Chancellor understands only too well that if the reduction of inflation today is not translated into the achievement of growth tomorrow the brave monetarist experiment with which he is so closely associated will have proved a deadly failure.

In July 1983 Mr Lawson introduced an emergency package of measures to reduce public borrowing by £1,000m in 1983-84. The move followed clear signs that government spending and borrowing were running well over target, pushing up money growth in the process. The Chancellor's action implies a more uncompromising approach than suggested here, at least on fiscal policy. But there is no sign as yet that he intends to tighten the screw further as opposed to endeavouring to steer the medium-term financial strategy back on course.

4 Facing up to the public spending Leviathan

Published June 22 1983

For many people the true test of Mr Nigel Lawson's tough reputation will be his ability to get to grips with the public spending Leviathan, which destroyed Tory hopes for tax cuts in Mrs Thatcher's first term and threatens to do so once again. But the new Chancellor is even more disadvantaged than his predecessor, Sir Geoffrey Howe. He must combat the monster, now bigger than ever, with one hand tied behind his back, the result of battles already fought and lost.

Over the four years between 1979 and 1983, public spending in real terms – after adjusting for inflation – has risen by 6 per cent, swallowing 44 per cent of national income compared with 40.5 per cent in 1979-80. The massive post-Clegg public sector pay awards the government honoured in its first year of office, the costs imposed by deepening recession – higher social security payments, state industry subsidies, special employment measures – and Conservative pledges to raise spending on defence and law and order all combined to drive up the overall total at a time when the economy was shrinking.

The magnitude of the task facing Mr Lawson was spelled out by a secret Treasury memorandum on public spending to the end of the decade sent to the Cabinet in autumn 1982. This predicted that even if the economy grew by about 2.5 per cent a year – 'not far short of the best we can expect' – leading to a drop in unemployment to two million by 1990, public spending would still gobble up the same proportion of the national cake as in 1979. If on the other hand the economy were to endure prolonged stagnation, with growth averaging 0.5 to 0.75 per cent a year, public spending would rise to 47 per cent of output. That, Sir Geoffrey said in his accompanying memorandum, would entail tax increases of £15,000m – equivalent to raising income tax to 45p in the pound.

The government's spending plans to 1985-86 assume growth of 2.5 per cent a year and no further rise in unemployment, broadly in line with the more cheerful long-term scenario. Total spending remains roughly constant in real terms. On this basis, according to the 1983 Budget statement, public borrowing could fall to 2 per cent of national output from more than 3 per cent in 1982-83 and still leave room for a 4 to 5p cut in the basic rate of income

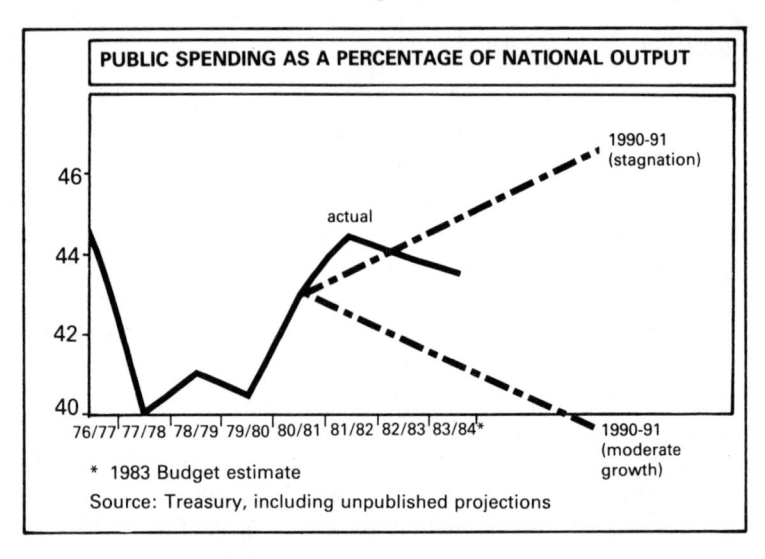

PUBLIC SPENDING AS A PERCENTAGE OF NATIONAL OUTPUT

* 1983 Budget estimate
Source: Treasury, including unpublished projections

tax. Mrs Thatcher's dream of slashing the rate to 25p in the £ would be within a whisker of fulfilment, well in time for the next election.

Yet it is hard to find anyone outside government who believes this is on the cards. The government's targets in past years have repeatedly been blown off course and there is every reason to fear that similar upsets lie in wait for Mr Lawson. To start with, the Conservatives are pledged to increase large hunks of spending: defence, which is planned to rise by 3 per cent in real terms in line with NATO requirements; law and order; health, where demographic pressures alone add nearly 1 per cent to real spending each year; and pensions and other social benefits where spending is determined by the (increasing) numbers who qualify. These four categories account for nearly 60 per cent of the total. Whatever the public spending plans may now say, the chance of offsetting cuts in the remaining programmes is slender. There is not much fat left to trim.

This is before questioning the government's assumptions on growth and unemployment. The majority of independent forecasters are predicting that the recovery will start to fizzle out in 1984, with growth thereafter too slow to stop the number of jobless from rising. The consequence once again would be to push up government spending and cut revenues, making a further rise in taxes inevitable if borrowing is held down.

Mr Walter Eltis, writing for stockbrokers Rowe and Pitman, has calculated that 1.5 per cent growth would be required just to keep tax rates unchanged while leaving room for some reduction in borrowing. To make any significant cut in taxation the government would need growth of at least 2.5 per cent a year, enough to start bringing unemployment down.

Sir Geoffrey himself expressed doubts on whether recovery could be sustained when he told the Cabinet in 1982 that 'we must not make the mistake of assuming that faster growth will float us over the rocks'. (The government of course remains strongly opposed to the use of expansionist policies to keep the economy moving.) The rates of taxation implied by the slow growth scenario 'would plainly be quite unacceptable', Sir Geoffrey wrote. 'This calls in my view for some thorough study and new insights, leading at a later stage to radical decisions, affecting most if not all of the major programmes. We cannot neglect any possible approach.'

But there is no sign that ministers, for all their fine words, are prepared to contemplate the wholesale butchery of the public sector that would be required. Indeed the options put up by the government's now-disbanded Think Tank (the Central Policy Review Staff) to accompany the long-term spending projections so shocked the Cabinet that it refused to discuss them. Subsequent attempts by the Prime Minister, with the backing of the Treasury, to resurrect the Think Tank report have backfired. Education vouchers and student loans have been shelved as impracticable and costly. Financing the health service through private insurance has been rejected by Mr Norman Fowler, the Health and Social Services Secretary, after a Whitehall study. The government is pledged to maintain the real value of state pensions – almost half all social security spending – while attempts to cut the real value of other benefits would undoubtedly attract the maximum of political odium from both sides of the House of Commons for the minimum of cash savings. That leaves defence, where the Think Tank simply suggested that the share of defence in national output might be frozen when Britain's NATO commitment to increase spending expires in 1985-86.

When Mrs Thatcher asked government departments to report to her by Easter 1983 on ways in which they could reduce spending over the next ten years she drew a blank. She was told that no further cuts, above those already planned, were possible.

All this places Mr Lawson in an awkward position. Tough and combative though he may be, and dedicated to rolling back the frontiers of the state, there is a limit to the extent to which he can fight old battles over again. He is not left with much to play with – some tinkering at the edges of the health service (short of anything that could be described as dismantlement), perhaps some move to privatise pensions (though this would take many years to pay off in government savings), certainly the sale of state assets, notably British Telecom, British Airways and yet more council homes.

But if radical moves are ruled out, the Chancellor and Mr Peter Rees, his Chief Secretary, are going to have their work cut out simply to hold constant the real level of public spending. If the economy fails to grow even this may defeat their combined talents. Mr Lawson may do better to concentrate on how to keep recovery going than to lay about him with a blunted spending axe if Tory tax promises are to become reality.

5 The black hole in the economy

Published August 13 1982

How big is the 'black' or 'hidden' economy? Popular belief suggests it is very large indeed – if only because virtually everyone is involved in it, one way or another. To judge from some studies we are a nation of petty fiddlers and cheats – using work facilities for private business or 'borrowing' work equipment, working on the side for undeclared cash, 'forgetting' to tell the taxman about odd bits of income. And if we do not do this ourselves we all know or think we know people who do.

Sir Lawrence Airey, Chairman of the Board of Inland Revenue, caused quite a stir in 1981 when he admitted to the Public Accounts Committee that he paid his window cleaner in cash (though who is to say that the gentleman in question did not dutifully declare that sum to the taxman). Translating the wealth of anecdotal evidence into hard cash is however another matter. Estimates of the size of the black economy for this country range from 2 to 3 per cent of national income to 15 per cent. Sir Lawrence Airey himself has suggested that the black economy accounts for roughly 6 to 8 per cent of national income, equivalent to £15,000m and representing some £4,000m of lost tax revenue each year.

The economic implications of these lost revenues are far reaching. An extra £4,000m of taxes collected would, for instance, halve the public sector borrowing requirement which the government has been struggling to bring down; or enable it to slash 4p off the basic rate of income tax; or abolish the employers' national insurance surcharge and have money left over for a modest selective boost to public investment, as the Confederation of British Industry has urged.

There are various ways in which researchers have tried to calculate the size of the black economy, all of them indirect and none of them very satisfactory. One way is to try to spot discrepancies in statistics for the economy as a whole. For instance, the Central Statistical Office has used the difference between the (bigger) expenditure and income estimates of national output, on the assumption that spending is more likely

52 Economic Overview

to be picked up by official figures than the income that generates it. The CSO put the hidden economy at 3 to 4 per cent of national income in 1978. The trouble with this is that the difference between the two estimates also reflects other errors and omissions in the compilation of the figures, and later upward revisions to the income estimates since 1978 have substantially reduced the gap between them and the expenditure measure.

Another way of measuring the black economy is to look at what is happening to cash transactions, on the assumption that most concealed payments are made in cash. For instance, the disproportionate increase in the use of large denomination notes has been taken as evidence of a booming black economy. Between 1972 and 1978 the value of £10 and £20 notes in circulation rose by 470 per cent while the value of all notes rose by 110 per cent. But this can be just as easily explained by the impact of inflation on the amount of cash people have to carry around with them.

American studies have put the hidden economy in the United States at between 10 and 25 per cent of national output, by arguing that *changes* in the ratio of cash transactions to total transactions (or total transactions to national income) represent changes in the size of the hidden economy. The studies assume for convenience that the black economy did not exist before the war. Professor Edgar Feige of the University of Wisconsin, who applied this method to Britain, estimated the black economy at 15 per cent of national output, implying a loss of tax revenue of some £11,000m, rather more than the 1982-83 projected £9,500m public sector borrowing requirement.

But these estimates have been greeted with considerable scepticism by researchers here and abroad. A calculation using a similar method by the Institute for Fiscal Studies gave the intriguing result that the black economy had shrunk enormously since the early 1950s when it accounted for nearly a third of gross domestic product!

The Institute for Fiscal Studies itself decided on a 'bottom up' approach, by looking at the discrepancies between the income and spending recorded by households taking part in the government's Family Expenditure Survey. It concluded that the black economy accounted for no more than 2 to 3 per cent of national income, with the self-employed and to a lesser extent part-time workers most likely to be involved.

Since the self-employed have much more opportunity than

everyone else to conceal their income it is not surprising that survey after survey should point the finger at them as the main source of tax losses in Britain as elsewhere. In 1976 the General Secretary of the Inland Revenue Staff Federation complained that 'the low incomes to which the self-employed admit defy belief. Only 70,000 of them declare the average wage of £60 or more. Only 250,000 of them admit to more than £30 a week.' Yet self-employed people, FES data suggests, have much higher living standards than employees with the same recorded incomes.

How then does the Inland Revenue come by its much-quoted estimate of 6 to 8 per cent of GDP? Unlike its American counterpart, it has no powers to scrutinise taxpayers' affairs at random, a deficiency to which the Public Accounts Committee has drawn attention. It appears to have reached this figure by what one might call a 'plausibility' analysis. According to a recent study by the Organisation for Economic Cooperation and Development, the Inland Revenue prepared its 1977 estimate of the black economy – then put at 7.5 per cent of GDP – by taking different hypothetical levels of income under-reporting (15, 10, 5 per cent of GDP and so on) converting them to a sum per worker and selecting one that looked plausible. The final estimate for 1977 could 'plausibly have arisen' on the assumption that all two million self-employed people concealed an average £1,000 of income and that six million of the 23 million wage earners also concealed about £1,000 of earnings, mostly from moonlighting. The latest estimate of 6 to 8 per cent of national income was presumably prepared in a similar way.

The Inland Revenue is trying to clamp down on tax evasion with all the resources that civil service staff cuts will allow. But some at least of that lost tax is, as Sir Lawrence Airey put it to the Public Accounts Committee, 'fairy gold'. If the unreported income were taxed some people might not bother to go on earning it.

We do not know how big the black economy is nor whether it is growing or declining. But we do know that it is significant and a permanent feature of the national economy. The very first report of the Inland Revenue complained that in 1806 'it is notorious that persons living in easy circumstances, nay, even in apparent affluence, have returned their income under £60 (the then tax exemption limit), although their annual expenditure has been treble that sum, and to whom there was no ground for imputing extravagance.' Little has changed since then.

III Inflation and Unemployment

Introduction

When the Conservative government came to power in May 1979 it made the defeat of inflation its prime economic target. Prices were then increasing by more than 10 per cent a year and the rate was accelerating. Exacerbated by the decision in the government's first Budget to double VAT and by spiralling pay awards led by the public sector inflation soared to a peak of 22 per cent a year later, but then fell with little interruption to less than 4 per cent in June 1983 when Mrs Thatcher was re-elected for a second term.

The government has set its sights on price stability as an ultimate objective and appears determined to make some progress towards that goal over the next few years. At the same time it has disclaimed responsibility for maintaining a high level of employment in the economy, arguing that if workers press for higher wages than its disinflationary money and fiscal policies allow for they have only themselves to blame for the resulting unemployment. Since 1979 the number of jobless has soared from 1.2 million or 5 per cent of the workforce to around 3 million (13 per cent) in 1983. The number of long-term unemployed has risen faster still. In October 1983 well over one million people had been out of work for more than a year, 30 per cent of them aged under 25, compared with 350,000 in April 1979. Put very crudely, a drop in inflation from an underlying rate of 12 to 13 per cent in 1979 has been achieved at the cost of about two million extra unemployed – about 1 per cent off inflation for every 250,000 made jobless. It will take a long time for these people to find work again. This extra unemployment is

a semi-permanent cost of the reduction in inflation.
The government did not set out deliberately to create unemployment of this dimension, nor did it anticipate the severity of the world recession which followed (and which may have been responsible for perhaps half the rise in the number of jobless). It believed the advice of monetarist economists who said the costs to the real economy of reducing inflation through strict monetary control would be small, because people would quickly moderate price and wage demands. The important thing was for the policy to be credible. But it soon became clear that behaviour did not respond to the announcement of monetary targets. Instead it changed slowly and unevenly as tight financial policies deepened recession and drove up unemployment.

The impact on unemployment was more than past experience would have suggested. Companies shed workers at an unprecedented rate in their fight to survive the financial squeeze and, as production began to revive, showed singular reluctance to take them on again. Partly, this must reflect lack of confidence in future demand prospects. But it also reflects the costliness of labour. The rise in labour costs over the past decade or so has far outstripped the growth of productivity. The result has been a significant increase in the real cost of employing labour and a fall in the share of national income going to profits, on which future investment and economic growth depend. The increased share of labour has been especially marked in manufacturing, where the vast majority of the jobs lost in the post-1979 recession have been concentrated.

Higher labour costs have undoubtedly discouraged firms from hanging on to workers and recruiting more. As a result some unemployment, perhaps a substantial amount, would remain even if the government were to reflate the economy because companies would not find it worthwhile to take people on. There is thus some sense in ministers' claims that workers must 'price themselves back into jobs'. But where they emphasise cuts in real wages, others prefer to concentrate on how to boost growth and productivity. Both strategies reduce unit labour costs. But the first puts the whole burden of adjustment on living standards; the second does not.

Monetarists call in support the notion of the 'natural rate of unemployment' – sometimes called the NAIRU or non-accelerating inflation rate of unemployment. This is defined as the jobless rate at which the inflation rate is steady. If unemployment is higher than the natural rate, wage and price inflation will fall; if unemployment is lower, it will accelerate. Monetarists argue that there is no trade-off in the long run between the two. The government can choose the rate of inflation through controlling money growth. After a period of transition – when policies to reduce inflation may temporarily lead to higher unemployment – it will always return to its natural level.

The natural rate is determined by structural or 'supply-side' factors in the economy, and cannot be shifted by pumping in more demand. It has risen in recent years, so adherents believe, because growing trade union power has pushed up employment costs, increased social security benefits relative to wage levels have encouraged people to stay on the dole rather than accept lower wages, and rigidities in the housing market, especially the inability of council tenants easily to move home, have stopped people from looking for work elsewhere.

This is one of the most important reasons why the government has introduced union reform, cut the value of social security benefits and pursued an aggressive council house sales policy. The government clearly hopes that in lowering the natural rate it can pave the way for a simultaneous drop in both inflation and unemployment. As long as the number of jobless remains above the natural rate, even if it is falling, the theory suggests that downward pressure on inflation will continue.

What is disputed, even among monetarists, is how long it takes for unemployment to return to its natural rate. Some economists now fear that the 'short run' may last for several years, with each successive tightening of policy to bring inflation down further risking a fresh 'temporary' rise in the number of jobless. Attempts to lower the natural rate itself are likely to be effective only in the long run. Keynesians, on the other hand, have never subscribed to the natural rate hypothesis. They believe that the way modern mixed economies work means that without an incomes policy there is a permanent unemployment/inflation trade-off. Thus the pursuit of still lower inflation will mean that unemployment goes on rising, though perhaps less steeply than before.

Keynes himself did not address the problem of long-run inflation and wage bargaining behaviour. 'One is also, simply because one knows no solution, inclined to turn a blind eye to the wages problem in a full employment economy' he wrote in 1945. Before the war prices often fell, as they did in the depression of the 1930s. After the war they rose continuously. The government's commitment to running the economy at full employment meant the price of resources, including labour, was bid up. Experience of uninterrupted inflation bred additional pressures on costs and prices, notably on the wages front. The loss of money illusion and expectations of future inflation led trade unions to press for real wage increases which themselves pushed up prices and set off a price-wage spiral. Free collective bargaining, much of it at plant level, produced leap-frogging claims which then sparked off demands for parity elsewhere. Employers conceded pay deals which were not justified by productivity improvements because they knew they could pass all or most of the extra cost on in prices. In the 1960s inflation began to accelerate, and during the 1970s it was rarely in single figures.

Despite the government's recent success in bringing inflation down to low levels the nature of the pay bargaining system, including the growth of the trade unions, and the cumulative effects of the post-war experience, means that inflationary psychology is deeply embedded in the economic system. Up to now, pressures on prices have been restrained by high unemployment or, sporadically over the last 20 years, by incomes policies. The government has yet to demonstrate that neither are necessary to stop inflation taking off once more.

Nevertheless, ministers have shifted the ground of debate. When inflation was in double-digits there were plenty of people who maintained that because the costs of reducing inflation were so heavy it would be better to learn to live with it. But now that the rate is in low single figures it is hard to find anyone prepared to defend significantly higher inflation even as a necessary accompaniment to more employment.

The fact is that inflation is unpopular. And there are good reasons for thinking that rapid inflation may be bad for growth, chiefly because uncertainty over future returns will tend to inhibit industrial investment. Although perfectly anticipated inflation should have few if any economic costs it is arguable that inflation is more variable (and so less easy to anticipate) when it is high than when it is low. In addition, inflation redistributes income haphazardly and so tends to heighten social friction.

There is more doubt, however, over whether aiming for price stability is a sensible aim of policy, especially if it involves the loss of more jobs. Zero inflation means that changes in relative wages and prices, which are necessary in a market economy, necessitate some cuts in money terms, cuts which on past form could well meet with substantial resistance.

Most of the pieces in this section were written some time ago, when inflation had yet to come firmly under control and unemployment was rising steeply towards three million. The first, 'Should we learn to live with inflation?' discusses the validity of the government's belief that inflation 'causes' unemployment. The second, 'Will recovery put paid to lower inflation?', outlines the arguments on both sides of the Keynesian/monetarist divide. The gloomy prospects for putting the unemployed back to work over the next few years are the subject of 'A hard road back to full employment', while 'Does cheaper labour mean more jobs' looks at the debate over real wages. The problems of defining and counting the unemployed are examined in 'Playing the jobless numbers game', and the panoply of special employment and training measures in 'Job schemes: only second best'.

A notable omission is any article on direct restraint of incomes. This has simply failed to surface as an issue in the unemployment/inflation debate. The government has vigorously rejected any suggestion of a formal incomes policy – though it keeps a firm grip on public sector pay – nor has it been prepared to enter into understandings with the trade unions. It believes that the unions have progressively exploited governments' commitment to maintain full employment and reneged on their side of the bargain. It also believes that incomes policies soon become unworkable by distorting market mechanisms and earnings differentials, and by provoking catch-up settlements which leave pay and inflation the same or worse than they would have been without the incomes policy.

Supporters of incomes policy, of course, believe that it could provide a way of lessening the unemployment costs of the move to lower inflation. They have come up with a number of ingenious designs, including an inflation tax on firms (which would tax companies which gave workers pay rises over the agreed norm), and a new kind of arbitration tribunal (which would decide wage claims on the basis of what would promote employment). But the government has turned a resolutely deaf ear to such proposals and incomes policy is unlikely to surface as a live issue until the next election.

1 Should we learn to live with inflation?

Published March 15 1982

The Treasury's model of the economy suggests that using tight money policies to slow inflation each 1 per cent fall in the annual inflation rate costs over four years the equivalent of 4 per cent of one year's gross domestic product and an extra year's unemployment for 2.5 per cent of the labour force. Is reducing the rate of inflation really so important as to make these costs worthwhile?

The government has argued that, in the long-run, there is no trade-off between more inflation and more unemployment. On the contrary, it believes, inflation causes unemployment. Bringing the rate down to low levels is a pre-condition of sustained economic growth and prosperity.

In Britain high inflation and low growth have seemingly gone together in recent years. But the international picture is a mixed one. Some countries (Belgium, Germany, Japan) have combined low inflation rates with high growth. Others have experienced

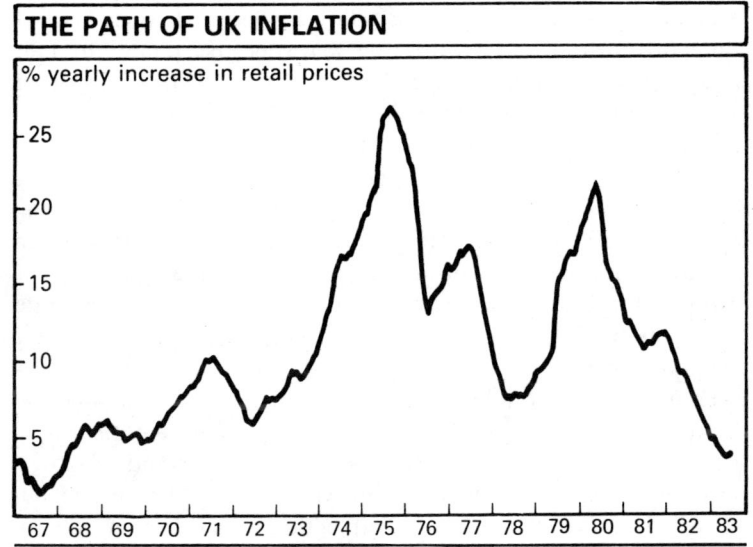

THE PATH OF UK INFLATION

% yearly increase in retail prices

Source: Department of Employment

rapid inflation and high growth (Brazil and Israel) or low inflation and low growth (the United States and Switzerland).

In what sense then can inflation be held to cause unemployment? Roger Bootle, economist with stockbrokers Capel-Cure Myers, writing in the December 1981 issue of the *Three Banks Review*, suggests five possible mechanisms, only three of which he considers to have some validity.

First, inflation causes unemployment because governments try to deal with it by deflationary policies which cause unemployment. This, however, simply begs the question at issue, which is why inflation is so harmful that painful remedies are required.

Secondly, it is argued that inflation produces a shift from profits to wages, as workers secure higher pay rises than the firm can recoup through price increases. This leads to lower investment and to cutbacks in the number of workers firms employ. Such a shift has undoubtedly taken place over the last ten years or so but this is just as likely to be a cause of inflation – as workers attempt to increase their incomes at the expense of profits – as a consequence of it. Deflationary policies, which rely on squeezing company finances in order to screw down wages, in fact make this 'profits pinch' more severe.

Thirdly, and more convincingly, inflation which is more rapid than that of trade rivals, causes loss of competitiveness which leads to job losses in industries squeezed by imports at home or in export markets abroad. Bootle argues that this loss of competitiveness can be offset by allowing the pound to fall, though past experience suggests that much of the benefit of depreciation is nullified by the attempts of wage-earners to recoup losses in real income. However, far from trying to improve competitiveness, this government attempted to bring down inflation by deliberately allowing the pound to rise during 1979 and 1980 with devastating consequences for industry. Even countries with an excellent inflation record, such as Germany or Switzerland, have lost competitiveness through exchange rate appreciation. So lower inflation is no *guarantee* of greater competitiveness.

Fourthly, inflation leads to uncertainty about real financial rewards. For example, a worker with a 10 per cent pay rise could see a big fall in living standards, unchanged standards or a substantial increase, depending on whether inflation turned out to be 15, 10 or 5 per cent, and without any certain way of knowing in advance. One of the most damaging effects of this

Inflation and Unemployment 61

uncertainty is that businesses hold back on investment because the real return (and the real cost of the money they may need to borrow) is unpredictable. This depresses employment. However, there is no firm evidence that uncertainty is greater when inflation is higher. Reducing the average level of inflation by a few per cent may not mean the rate is less variable.

Finally, inflation may depress consumption and thus employment because people save more to restore the real value of their money savings – the wealth effect. But most models of the economy suggest this effect is not very powerful, while deflationary policies which depress consumption are, in any event, a perverse response.

All this indicates, according to Roger Bootle, that inflation causes unemployment only to the extent that it changes relative values unfavourably (or creates uncertainty about relative values) between groups or between countries. But deflationary policies designed to bring down the average rate of inflation do little to ameliorate this central problem, while inflicting considerable damage of their own.

A number of economists share his view that it is not inflation as such that causes problems but the fact that it is imperfectly anticipated. This leads, for instance, to arbitrary shifts of income and wealth from creditors to debtors – including redistribution from old people living on savings to young people borrowing to set up home, and from households who lend the government money by buying gilts to the government which sees the real value of its debt falling.

The solution, these economists believe, is not to agonise over reducing inflation but to improve anticipation of price rises by widespread use of indexation for incomes, financial contracts and so on. Then the only costs will be the relatively insignificant administrative ones of changing price labels and the like. 'Provided that the costs of even perfectly anticipated inflation are not great, there is a good case for trying to cope with inflation by improving the degree to which inflation is anticipated, and ensuring that all parts of the economy are allowed to adjust to it', Roger Bootle argues.

There are even some economists, though fewer than there used to be, who believe that inflation has some positive benefits. In particular, it provides an automatic reconciliation of the battle between competing groups for a higher share of national output. This argument lost some of its force during the 1970s because experience of rapid inflation led to the final loss of 'money illusion'. All groups are now wise to the fact that inflation erodes living standards. The distributional struggle is seen increasingly for what it is, without the prospect of rapid economic growth to square the circle by giving to the poor without taking from the rich.

In a country without sufficient authority to compel a particular distribution of income, or sufficient consensus about what it should be, a tendency towards continuing and perhaps accelerating inflation may be inevitable. That is why many economists, not by any means hard-line monetarists, share with the government the belief that inflation must be controlled if the economy is to grow on a sustainable basis. They see the choice not as one between a high steady rate and a low steady rate but as one between a steady rate and an accelerating one.

A policy of deflation, however, fails to tackle the underlying causes of inflation. It exacerbates the distributional conflict and does little to improve the pay bargaining system which encourages unrealistic pay claims. When demand revives, inflation is all too likely to pick up again, perhaps worse than before, as workers seek compensation for lost living standards and companies try to restore eroded profit margins. Either we accept inflation and adjust to it as best we can, as some other high-inflation countries have done, or we tackle it at source by attempting, through an incomes policy or otherwise, to bring a degree of consensus into the process of fixing incomes.

The most worrying feature of the government's present strategy is, as Roger Bootle says, 'the dreadful prospect that granted success against inflation, granted even continuing success, after all we have been through, and with a now much weaker economic base, the underlying problems of the British economy would remain much as they were, almost unaffected by what the government would regard as a tremendous achievement.'

Subsequent events make this article appear overly pessimistic about the benefits of reducing inflation. In particular, later evidence suggests that higher inflation does tend to be more variable than lower inflation, so increasing uncertainty. And the wealth effect has turned out to be a much more powerful mechanism for stimulating consumption than most economists predicted. While inflationary psychology has not been broken, expectations of future inflation have come down decisively. It remains to be seen whether expectations will revive as the economy picks up.

2 Will recovery put paid to lower inflation?

Published October 27 1982

The extraordinary drop in the inflation rate since the beginning of 1982 caught that élite band of economists, the forecasters, on the hop. In March, with inflation in double figures, they were sceptical at the prospect of achieving 9 per cent inflation by the end of the year. In July, when the Chancellor, Sir Geoffrey Howe, predicted that inflation would fall to 7.5 per cent by Christmas, many reacted with disbelief. But by the autumn, as each successive monthly figure showed the yearly pace of price rises tumbling, City forecasters have vied to beat the Treasury in optimism. Already the Chancellor's most recent forecast of 6.5 per cent before the year is out is widely regarded as too high (a view shared by the Treasury) and some cheerful souls are talking in terms of little more than 5 per cent.[1]

As for next year forecasters are daring to think about what just a few months ago would have been unthinkable – a return to price stability. Even before the Chancellor announced in his Mansion House speech last week that inflation would fall to 5 per cent next spring – a level last seen in 1970 – Buckmaster and Moore, the stockbrokers, were bruiting the possibility that prices in May 1983 would be no higher than those of a year earlier. 'The effect on a generation almost tranquillised on a diet of inflation could be traumatic', the firm says. As Mr Colin Mitchell, its research partner, points out: 'It is something that has not been seen since the 1930s, and will affect people in every aspect of

1 They were right in the end. The actual figure was 5.5 per cent.

City Forecasts of Inflation

Forecast for (dated)	end-1982 (August 1982)	end-1982	spring 1983 (October 1982)	end-1983	end-1983	spring 1984 (November 1983)	end-1984
James Capel	7.7	6.5	5.5	6.0	5.1	6.0	4.5
Simon and Coates	8.2	6.7	5.7	6.7	5.8	6.6	6.7
Messels	7.5	5.4	4.0	n.a.	5.3	5.3	4.8
Laing and Cruickshank	7.6	6.5	6.0	7.5	5.6	6.2	6.0
Phillips and Drew	8.2	7.0	6.3	6.1	5.4	6.7	6.3
Grieveson Grant	7.5	7.0	6.5	6.7	5.7	7.0	5.8
Treasury	7.5	6.5	5	n.a	5	5.5	4.5

their lives, including their attitudes towards spending, saving, borrowing and pay.'

Since the scepticism which greeted earlier inflation forecasts proved so ill-founded, it would be foolhardy to dismiss lightly the chances of a further dramatic slowdown in price rises. But the consensus, shared by the Treasury, is that after falling to a low of 4.5 to 5 per cent in the second quarter of 1983 the inflation rate is likely to drift up slightly to between 6 and 7 per cent by the end of the year.[1]

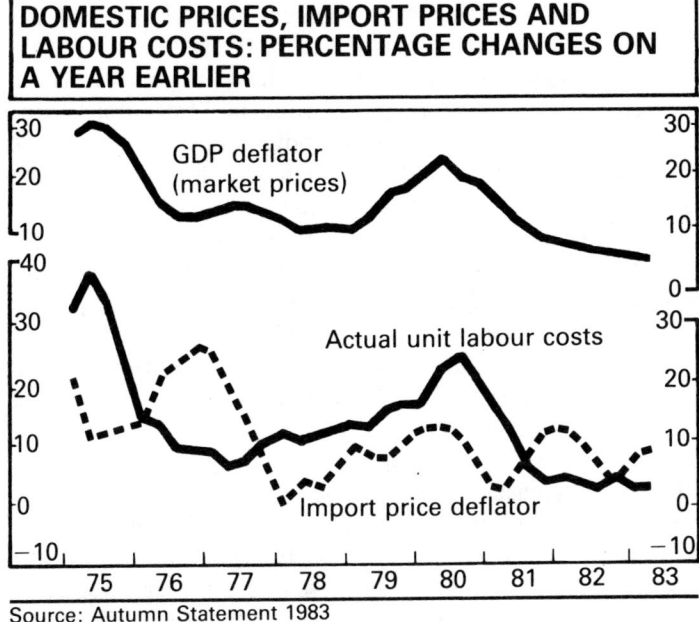

DOMESTIC PRICES, IMPORT PRICES AND LABOUR COSTS: PERCENTAGE CHANGES ON A YEAR EARLIER

GDP deflator (market prices)

Actual unit labour costs

Import price deflator

Source: Autumn Statement 1983

Whatever the short-term ups and downs of the inflation rate, it seems clear that there has been a decisive shift to lower inflation and lower inflationary expectations in the past year or so. No one expects prices to take off again as they did in the mid-1970s. The disagreements tend to centre around whether prices in the future will be rising in the below 5 per cent a year range, as the Chancellor clearly hopes, or in the 5 to 10 per cent a year range, as the less sanguine expect.

1 Inflation fell to a low of 3.7 per cent in May and June 1983, and subsequently rose gently. At the time of writing (November 1983) prices were expected to rise by 5 to 5.5 per cent in the twelve months to December 1983.

Inflation has come down much more rapidly than expected because of two main factors: the severe recession, in Britain and worldwide, and the overvalued pound. The high value of the pound helps inflation directly by cheapening the cost of imports, including raw materials bought by industry. And it helps indirectly by forcing companies to slash prices and profit margins to survive in world markets and to compete with imports at home. To this has been added the beneficial impact of weak commodity prices – now at their lowest level in real terms since 1950 – and soft oil prices because of the world recession. At home, massive and rising unemployment has kept pay deals down with workers fearing for their jobs.

Many, perhaps most, economists believe it is only a matter of time before these gains are put into reverse. Economic recovery means a relaxation of pressures on both companies and workers. With the threat of redundancy no longer hanging over them, workers may push for catch-up settlements to compensate for squeezed living standards over the past two years. Firms will try to rebuild profit margins, while improved cash flow could make them less resistant to higher pay claims. Commodity prices, as the Bank of England recently pointed out, are at unsustainably low levels and are bound to pick up as the world emerges from recession. The pound is set for a fall, as the balance of payments worsens, pushing up import costs once more and easing the competitive squeeze on companies.

Others – Treasury officials among them – see things differently. With economic recovery likely to remain sluggish at best, unemployment will stay high and firms will still be under strong pressure to hold costs down. In these circumstances, according to this view, workers are unlikely to get pay rises substantially in excess of inflation. If inflation rates go on falling, the general level of pay settlements should follow suit, since smaller pay rises are needed to maintain living standards. In addition, as output recovers, productivity should rise more rapidly, largely offsetting the cost of higher wage deals. So firms would need relatively modest price increases to rebuild profit margins. World prospects, too, look dull over the next few years. Tight money and fiscal policies by the leading industrial countries and the contraction of bank lending to the developing nations have seen to that. So commodity prices are unlikely to rise by much. Even if the pound does fall in the coming months, tumbling inflation round the world means the inflation risks are much less than they would have been only two years ago.

Given the depressed outlook for the world economy over the next few years, the balance of the argument would seem for the moment at least to rest with those who expect inflation to drop to very low levels. This will last as long as the main industrial countries, including Britain, continue to regard achieving a low and stable rate of inflation as the principal object of policy and are prepared to bear the cost in terms of sluggish growth and high unemployment.

Certainly, the present British government has made clear that price stability is its ultimate objective. Though the Chancellor may be reluctant to hurry in that direction next year in the run-up to the election, the re-election of Mrs Thatcher would be a mandate for continuation of tough anti-inflation policies until the goal is reached. What has not been achieved, however, is a way of reconciling low inflation with rapid growth and falling unemployment. The fear must be that, for Britain at least, we must choose one or the other but cannot have both at the same time, with the consequence that in the long run neither course can be sustained.

The performance of inflation since this article was written tends to bear out the Treasury's case. Pay settlements have come down slowly – but inflation has fallen faster, with the result that for those in work living standards have risen sharply.

Between September 1982 and September 1983 earnings increased by 7.5 per cent but prices rose by only 5 per cent. The government's official Tax and Price Index, which measures the rise in gross pay needed to maintain the purchasing power of take-home pay, rose by even less because of tax cuts in the 1983 Budget – up by 4 per cent in the twelve months to September.

But relatively high pay deals have not forced industry to put up its prices by the same amount because rapid improvements in productivity have kept wage costs per unit of output down.[1] Companies have been able to boost profits substantially, despite higher costs of fuel and raw materials

1 See chart on p. 74.

as the pound declined and world commodity prices spurted with the upturn in the global economy at the start of 1983.

Broader measures of inflation, such as the GDP deflator that measures price increases across the domestic economy, which are less distorted than the retail prices index by import costs and changes in the mortgage rate, suggest that the underlying trend is still on a gently declining path.

3 A hard road back to full employment

Published March 30 1981

Economists divide themselves into two camps – the deeply pessimistic and the despairing – when it comes to forecasts of unemployment over the next ten years or so.

The pessimistic, who include such supporters of the present government's economic strategy as the London Business School's Centre for Economic Forecasting, see unemployment well above two million for the foreseeable future. The despairing, most of whom have little confidence in government policy, expect unemployment to rise well beyond three million and to stay at those chastening heights indefinitely in the absence of a major reversal of policy. Even with such a reversal the outlook for unemployment remains grim. Must we then abandon all hope of achieving low jobless levels throughout the 1980s or beyond?

For more than three decades after the end of the Second World War governments shared the view that society had a prime – some would argue paramount – duty to provide jobs for all its citizens who wished to work. This consensus persisted even when unemployment was deliberately being created as a weapon in the authorities' largely unsuccessful struggle to combat inflation. But it broke down completely in 1979 with the election of a Conservative government committed to monetarist economic policies, which denied that governments could influence unemployment levels over the long term. The defeat of inflation supplanted full employment as the overriding objective of policy.

UNEMPLOYMENT AND VACANCIES, UNITED KINGDOM

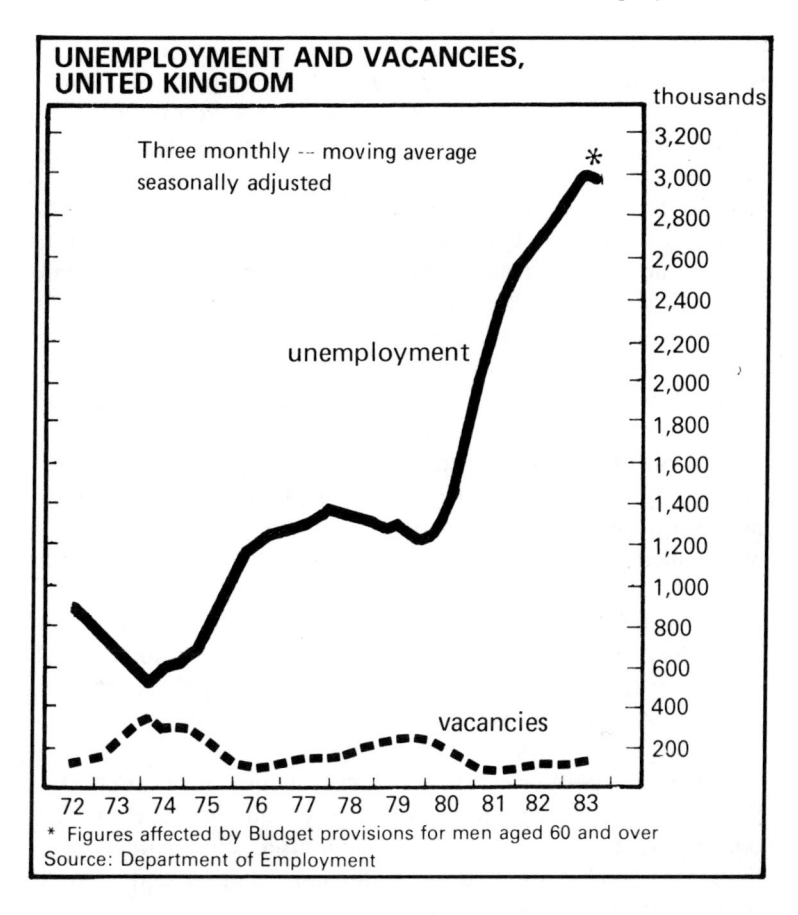

Three monthly – moving average seasonally adjusted

[Chart showing unemployment (solid line) rising from ~800 thousand in 1972 to over 3,000 thousand by 1983, and vacancies (dashed line) remaining low throughout, in thousands, from 1972 to 1983.]

* Figures affected by Budget provisions for men aged 60 and over
Source: Department of Employment

Monetarists believe that there is a 'natural rate' of unemployment in the economy, defined as the rate compatible with a constant inflation rate. What that constant inflation rate is depends on the growth of the money supply.

The natural unemployment rate at any time is determined by structural features of the economy and, more especially, by the labour market, including the level of unemployment benefit relative to income in work, workers' ability to move to where the jobs are (which in turn depends on conditions in the housing market) and willingness to accept lower pay rates to increase job prospects. In a paper for the Treasury and Civil Service Select Committee of MPs published last Wednesday the Treasury put the natural rate of unemployment at about 5 per cent of the workforce, equivalent to nearly 1.25 million unemployed adults.

70 *Inflation and Unemployment*

This is much higher than previous estimates in the mid-1970s which put the rate at 500,000 to 700,000 unemployed. But it may well be an underestimate. Dr Alan Budd of the London Business School, for example, believes that the rate may lie somewhere between 1.5 and 2 million.

According to the monetarist view, unemployment above the natural rate means that inflation will start to slow down as workers accept lower pay settlements and 'price themselves into work'. This process will also bring unemployment down gradually towards the natural rate. Unemployment below the natural rate produces steadily accelerating inflation and unemployment rises as workers 'price themselves out of work'. So it is no good governments trying to cut the number of jobless by boosting demand in the economy artificially. This may cut unemployment in the short run, but in the longer run (two to three years or more) injections of cash into the system simply add to inflation while unemployment returns inexorably to the same levels as before.

Governments can, of course, try to reduce the natural rate of unemployment by tackling the structural conditions which determine it – work incentives, housing reform or reduction of trade union power. This the present administration has attempted to do, so far with notable lack of success.

Post-war experience does not, however, give much support to the 'natural rate' hypothesis. It suggests, on the contrary, that boosts to demand do have a permanent effect on unemployment, though at some cost in terms of higher inflation and a worse balance of payments. A 3p in the £ cut in income tax, for example, costing £3,000m in 1983, would boost national output by about 1 per cent and create around 200,000 extra jobs within two or three years, according to the Treasury's model of the economy. This would knock rather fewer off the unemployment total because the labour force is still growing[1] and some of the people taking jobs would not have been included in the official jobless count. It would add under half a percentage point to the annual inflation rate.

The surges in unemployment over the past fifteen years or so – in 1967, 1971, 1975-76 and 1980-81 – have all resulted from deflationary policies pursued by governments which have deliberately chosen to put inflation or balance of payments objectives before the provision of employment.

1 By an estimated 150,000 a year between 1981 and 1986.

Inflation and Unemployment 71

But to bring unemployment in 1984 down from forecast levels (3.5 million or more[1] to present figures (2.3 million in March 1981), let alone to produce a fall below two million, would require the creation of 500,000 jobs a year between now and then, with a fiscal stimulus of some £7,500m each year. An increase in employment on that scale has not been achieved in this country since demobilisation. To bring unemployment down below one million, which many people would say is still too high, would, at more modest rates of job creation, take at least ten years.

Nor are the omens propitious for substantially increasing industrial employment over the next few years. World trade is expected to grow fairly slowly, depressing prospects for exports. And many people believe that the response of employment to changes in output may become increasingly sluggish as a result of improvements in productivity. If so, only enormous growth in the service industries, including public employment, could provide the extra jobs necessary to get unemployment down.

Also, surveys by the Confederation of British Industry and other evidence suggest that the present recession may have resulted in some permanent elimination of industrial capacity. So any expansion in demand could run into bottlenecks and shortages more quickly than in previous upturns. Further stimulus would then simply exacerbate inflation and suck in imports rather than give rise to additional jobs in domestic industries.

Of course, it is possible to devise combinations of measures which are rather more efficient in creating jobs than income tax cuts (which lead to substantial leakages through extra savings and imports), such as more public spending, or which minimise some of the side-effects, such as incomes policies. The creation of 200,000 new jobs a year – enough to start unemployment falling slowly – through sustained fiscal expansion over the next decade could probably be achieved without causing the economy to overheat. A £3,000m stimulus after all represents only 1 per cent of national output. But it is foolish to pretend that the costs will be negligible. The question is: is the price worth paying to avoid the continuing sacrifice of lives blighted by unemployment? Surveys of public opinion suggest that the majority of people in this country now believe that it is.

1 Forecasts made before changes in definition and policy which have, in total, taken more than half a million people out of the jobless count.

The government has stuck to its guns despite steadily rising unemployment. There has been no significant reflation of the economy – though both fiscal and monetary policy have been looser than planned, partly because of the sharp fall in inflation.

By late 1983, inflation was bobbing around 5 per cent, less than half 1981 levels, the economy was growing at about 3 per cent a year after a lengthy period of stagnation and the rise in unemployment had been halted, for the time being at least. The Treasury was predicting continuing growth, declining inflation, and stable unemployment in 1984.

Nevertheless, few economists expect unemployment to fall significantly in the foreseeable future, and many fear it may rise again before long as growth slows once more.

4 Does cheaper labour mean more jobs?

Published December 3 1981

One of the features of Mrs Thatcher's first term was a rerun of the Keynes-monetarist 'real wage' debate of the 1930s. Keynes, who then won the day, argued that cutting wages would not cure unemployment because, by reducing demand in the economy, it made recession worse. Workers could not 'price themselves into jobs' if industry had no need or desire to recruit them.

Now the monetarists have assumed the upper hand, arguing with some justification that steeply rising labour costs – which include not just wages but employers' national insurance contributions and the national insurance surcharge – have deterred employers from taking on workers.

No minister likes to play Scrooge when he can claim that his apparent meanness is really a concern for the welfare of those in his charge. Thus Treasury hawks, pressing for a savage cut in the real value of social security benefits, have argued that this is not simply to economise on public spending. The level of state benefits for the unemployed effectively sets a floor to wage rates, they suggest. Cutting the value of these benefits, thus exerting downward pressure on real wages in the economy, would also help workers 'to price themselves into jobs'. The basis for their belief lies in the seemingly obvious proposition that 'the more is charged for something the less will be bought'. So if the cost of employing people falls companies will, it is claimed, take on more workers.

The government has embraced this proposition with vigour. In his Mansion House speech in October the Chancellor, Sir Geoffrey Howe, speaking of obstacles to enterprise and wealth creation, told his audience: 'There is still much to be done, perhaps most of all in the labour market. We have to enable people, by encouraging them to be sensible about pay, to bring the price of their labour down to the level at which it can once again be fruitfully employed.'

The spearhead of the government's attack on real wages is its campaign, aided by high and rising unemployment and tough public sector cash limits, to talk down the level of pay settlements to well below the inflation rate. But the proposals for trade union reform, cuts in the real value of unemployment benefit, and the Young Workers Scheme – which will subsidise jobs for young people paid less than £45 a week[1] – are all weapons in its armoury.

Professor Patrick Minford of Liverpool University, an enthusiastic proponent of monetarist doctrine with some sympathisers in Whitehall, claims in his latest quarterly economic bulletin that reduction of trade union bargaining power through union reform alone would unleash the mechanisms 'to price hundreds of thousands of young people and long-term unemployed into work'.

These projections are viewed with some scepticism by opponents of the government's economic strategy. While conceding that cheaper labour might lead companies to employ more workers rather than, say, invest in labour-saving equipment, they argue that cuts in real wages may produce more unemployment by reducing demand in the economy through a reduction of consumer spending. In the short term this would almost certainly outweigh the beneficial but delayed impact on demand of

1 £47 a week or less in November 1983.

REAL LABOUR COSTS AND REAL EARNINGS: WHOLE ECONOMY LEVELS

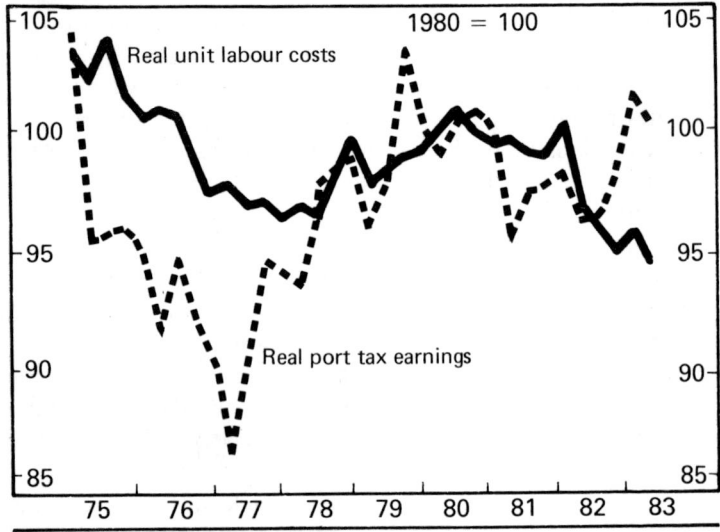

[Chart showing Real unit labour costs and Real port tax earnings, 1975–83, 1980 = 100]

Source: Autumn Statement 1983

improved international competitiveness. The consequence could be a deflationary spiral which would plunge the economy into ever-deeper recession.

The National Institute of Economic and Social Research, in its *Economic Review* published last week, described the argument that workers have priced themselves out of jobs as a 'grossly misleading simplification'. It placed the blame for unemployment squarely on lack of effective demand in the economy. But the Institute was prepared to concede that the share of profits in national output had been squeezed unduly, hurting investment and so growth and jobs. Not all of this has been caused by pressures from workers for more wages, however; the rising exchange rate, which automatically boosts real wages by lowering inflation, has also been to blame.

In addition, there can be a marked divergence between changes in workers' living standards (real wages after tax) and changes in employers' labour costs (which reflect before-tax pay plus employers' national insurance contributions and the surcharge). Over the past 20 years, after-tax real wages have risen by just over one-third; employers' labour costs have risen by two-thirds. Falling living standards may not be translated into extra jobs if the government increases taxes or other costs of employment.

Most economists agree that brighter job prospects ultimately depend on a reduction in real wages per unit of output to help boost competitiveness and profitability. But there are two dimensions to the problem – wages and output. The government is assuming that output is fixed (because it is not prepared to reflate the economy). So the whole burden of adjustment has to fall on real wages.

The government's adversaries, on the other hand, want to tackle the problem from the output end. If output is allowed to increase, they argue, productivity will rise. Real wages need not then fall, or not fall so much, to achieve the same objective.

In practice, real wage cuts may be unavoidable in the short term. Bringing down the rate of inflation invariably means curbing the rise in money wages. So wages will tend to fall behind the inflation rate until the rate itself comes down. Moreover, retrieving the huge loss of competitiveness over the past three years or so caused by rapid inflation and the rising exchange rate will necessitate some further fall in the value of sterling as well as low increases in domestic labour costs.

The point is that in the longer term, economic growth can sustain both rising real wages and falling unemployment. But growth is unlikely to materialise if real wages are depressed and no action is taken to stimulate the economy in other ways. Then the sacrifice of living standards could easily be in vain.

After peaking in 1980, the pace of earnings growth began to slow. Higher taxes and still rapid inflation contributed to a substantial decline in living standards, as measured by real after-tax earnings. But in 1982, with the rate of inflation tumbling and some easing of the tax burden, the living standards of those in work began to rise – by about 4 per cent in the pay round ending in August 1983.

Real unit labour costs, adjusted for inflation, after increasing between 1979 and 1980, began to fall, gently at first and then more steeply as productivity spurted ahead.

By 1983, with the economy picking up and productivity still improving rapidly, real unit labour costs were falling at the same time as workers' living standards were rising – a clear demonstration that economic growth accompanied by increased output per head can sustain both higher real wages and lower costs.

Recent work by the National Institute for Economic and Social Research confirms that real wages and labour costs can diverge sharply. Between 1979 and 1982, for instance, real take-home pay for the average worker went up by just 0.3 per cent. But the real cost of employing him rose by 4.4 per cent once the employers' national insurance contributions and the surcharge are taken into account. This was despite cuts in the surcharge from 3.5 to 1 per cent over that period.

In the decade to 1982, real after-tax earnings rose by only 4.5 per cent, less than 0.5 per cent a year. But the real cost of employing labour went up by 18.5 per cent. The proportion of the total accounted for by costs other than pay jumped from 11 to 15 per cent.

Lack of demand rather than higher 'real wages' lies behind the bulk of the steep increase in unemployment since 1979. But this does not mean the level of wages has no impact on job prospects. Research by the Department of Employment on young people's earnings, suggests that a rise in their earnings relative to those of adults does significantly reduce the number of jobs available to them – because it is less worthwhile for employers to take on untrained, inexperienced youngsters.

Between the mid-1960s and the mid-1970s boys' wages rose from about 45 per cent of men's to about 55 per cent, where they have broadly remained. Girls' wages in relation to women's stayed fairly steady at around 67 per cent over the same period. The Department of Employment argues that the high cost of employing youngsters has deprived them of job opportunities and exacerbated the impact of the recession, which has hit them hardest of all. Since 1979 the wages of young people have fallen slightly in relation to those of adults – but not by enough to have a big effect on job prospects.

A separate National Institute study also points out that British apprentices earn roughly three times as much relative to adult workers as in Germany and Switzerland – 60 per cent compared with 20 per cent – which has discouraged employers from offering enough training places to satisfy the demand.

5 Playing the jobless numbers game

Published December 3 1982

Mr Norman Tebbit, the Employment Secretary, was being decidedly disingenuous when he described the new system of collecting the unemployment figures, on which the November 1982 tally is based, as 'more accurate'. It will undoubtedly provide a highly precise up-to-date measure of the number of people claiming benefits at unemployment benefit offices. But it will be no more accurate, and arguably a great deal less so, than the old registration system at measuring the true number of people out of work in Britain.

The new system, based on a computerised count of benefit recipients, results from the move to voluntary registration for work at job centres, which means that since October 1982 counting the registered unemployed has ceased to be a reliable guide. Voluntary registration, which was recommended by Sir Derek Rayner, the Prime Minister's efficiency adviser, in the spring of 1981, is reckoned to save some £10 million a year (£2.5 million in the cost of collecting the statistics alone) and the jobs of 1,350 civil servants.

Cynics might claim that, savings notwithstanding, the government would not have gone ahead with the change if the consequence had been an extra quarter of a million added to the official jobless total. Instead, when the two counts were run in parallel for October 1982, the new system managed to cut the tally by 246,000 from 3.3 to 3.05 million. Although this was exceptionally large, the difference in previous months was generally between 170,000 and 190,000.

Three factors account for the difference. The first is that many unemployed people who registered for work do not claim benefit, mostly married women who do not qualify for it. In October this accounted for 161,000 of the discrepancy, roughly 100,000 of whom were married women. Secondly, the benefit offices are quicker at picking up and the computer at recording when people have found work than the manual count at job centres. This means that the old system included a lot of people who were in fact working – some 108,000 in October. It is this factor that gives rise to the Employment Department's claim that the new figures are 'more accurate'. Finally, the count includes for the first time about 23,000 severely disabled people. Summer school leavers, who do not qualify for social security benefits until September, will have to be counted separately.

Britain, like most other countries, uses whatever system of administration it has in effect to collect the jobless figures. These are bound to be imperfect. On the one hand, some of those out of work are not picked up by the system; on the other, some people recorded as unemployed may not be after jobs. Surveys suggest that about 400,000 people were looking for work but did not register as unemployed under the old system, while perhaps 50,000 jobless are getting sickness benefit who would otherwise be on the dole. A further 375,000 have been taken off the register by special employment and training measures, such as the Youth Opportunities Programme.[1] In addition, many more, married women in particular, will have given up the idea of looking for a job because the prospects of finding one are so poor – so-called 'discouraged workers'. After a generation in which an increasing proportion of women went out to work, often part-time, the rise has been halted. Women who would previously have sought jobs have dropped out of the labour market – though perhaps only temporarily. On past trends, half a million more women might be seeking work. Lastly, more people, especially men over 60, are retiring early, a trend which has accelerated in recent years.

Deciding how many of these people should be added to the unemployment tally is difficult. Strictly speaking, those now out of the labour force – the retired and discouraged workers – do not count as unemployed, even though they may have preferred to be in work. Early retirement, for instance, has been forced on many older workers, often in poor health, as firms cut back on jobs, and large numbers live close to the bread-line. On the other hand, many discouraged workers would undoubtedly take jobs were these to become available. And so, one suspects, would many of the newly self-employed – up by more than 200,000 between 1979 and 1981 after a decade of decline – who may well have branched out on their own for lack of any alternative. These people ought to be included.

1 400,000 in September 1983. The YOP has been superseded by the Youth Training Scheme.

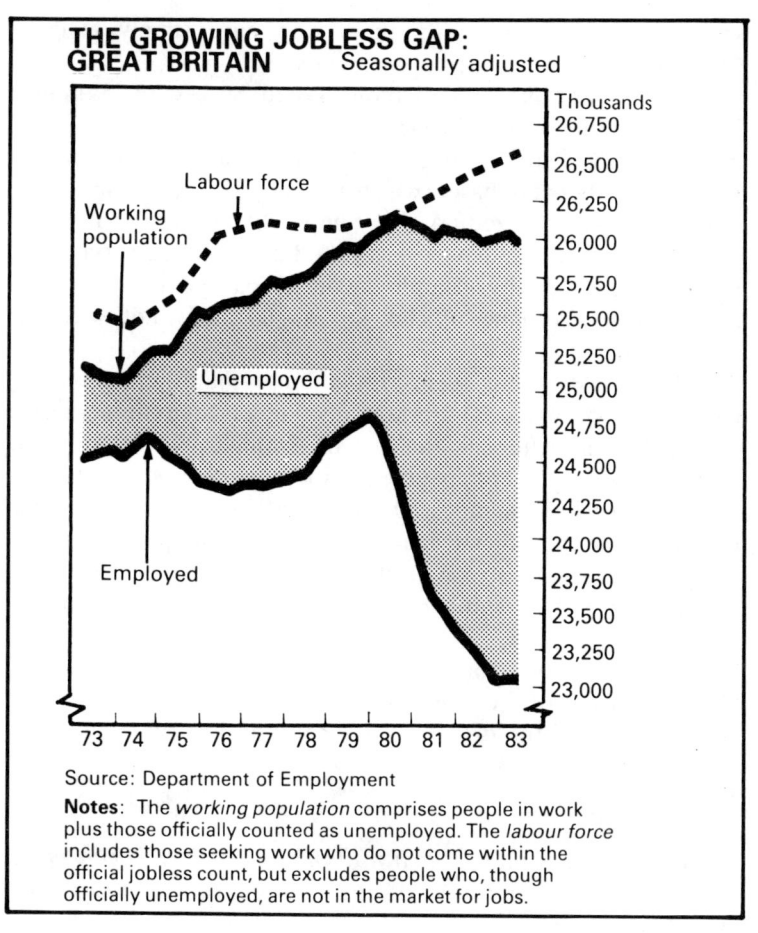

THE GROWING JOBLESS GAP:
GREAT BRITAIN   Seasonally adjusted

[Chart showing Working population / Labour force (dashed line) and Employed line, with Unemployed area between them, from 1973 to 1983. Y-axis in thousands from 23,000 to 26,750.]

Source: Department of Employment
Notes: The *working population* comprises people in work plus those officially counted as unemployed. The *labour force* includes those seeking work who do not come within the official jobless count, but excludes people who, though officially unemployed, are not in the market for jobs.

Adding to the new official jobless total the 120,000 or so people, mainly women, who previously registered for work but do not claim benefits, the 400,000 who surveys show are looking for work but did not register, the 50,000 unemployed sick, the 375,000 taken off the register by special employment schemes and, say, just 100,000 discouraged workers and the unwilling self-employed would take the number of unemployed in Britain to well over four million.

Against this the Employment Department claims that up to a fifth of those officially classed as unemployed – perhaps 400,000 people – are not, in fact, looking for work. They include people retiring early on occupational pensions (Mr Tebbit is fond of pointing to airline pilots and retired bankers as examples), those with a job to go to and others who have simply resigned themselves to permanent unemployment.

According to the 1981 Labour Force Survey, 2.35 million people said they were seeking work in spring 1981, whereas the number of registered jobless was 140,000 greater at 2.49 million. On the new benefits basis (which includes people claiming only national insurance credits) the comparable figure would have been 2.30 million – much closer to the Labour Force Survey, and another reason why Employment Department statisticians believe that the new official jobless count is not seriously misleading.

Nevertheless, there seems little doubt that the number of people out of work is substantially higher than the officially recorded level. After all, the fact that a high proportion of the long-term unemployed have ceased job-searching does not make them any the less unemployed. People looking for work but not picked up by the official figures, plus those on special employment schemes and so on, outweigh by a large margin those counted officially who do not consider themselves to be unemployed.

When the labour market improves, these hidden jobless will take their share of the work available. That is why, for every 70 people taken off the dole, at least 100 jobs must be created.

Since 1979 more than half a million people have been taken out of the official jobless count by changes in definition and special schemes.

In the autumn of 1981 men over 60 who had been on supplementary benefit for a year were allowed to opt for retirement and the higher long-term rate of benefit. Result: **minus 37,000.**

The change to a computerised count of people claiming benefits, instead of those registering at job centres, removed 170,000 to 190,000 from the official total from November 1982. Of these, however, about half were in jobs. Result: **minus 100,000.**

Hard on its heels came measures in the 1983 Budget to take more older men off the dole and into retirement. Result: **minus 160,000.**

And throughout the government's period of office the

scope and array of special employment and training measures, devised principally as a response to worsening joblessness, has burgeoned. At the last count in September 1983 they covered more than 600,000 people, most of them youngsters. That is well over double the number in May 1979.

The impact on the unemployment total is less than the numbers covered. But the latest estimates suggest that nearly 400,000 were taken off the dole as a result of the special measures, compared with 155,000 in spring 1979. Result: **minus 240,000.**

6 Job schemes: only second best

Published July 14 1981

The £1,000m package of measures which Mr James Prior, the Secretary of State for Employment, intends to put to Cabinet to take all school leavers out of the dole queue by 1983 is an understandable response to the horrific prospects for youth unemployment over the next few years. The number of school leavers who will not have found a job by the Christmas of the year in which they leave is expected to rise to nearly half a million by the end of 1983, more than double the 1980 total, and equivalent to roughly two in every three leavers.

That joblessness among youngsters has reached explosive proportions is surely no longer in doubt after the disturbances of Brixton, Toxteth and Moss Side. In January 1981, one in five under the age of 19 was registered as unemployed, accounting for a fifth of all those out of work.[1] 'By the end of 1983, only 40 per cent of the labour force aged under 18 will be in employment, compared with 70 per cent in 1980; while over 40 per cent will have had no experience of employment,' the Manpower Services

---

1 In October 1983 the proportion of 16- to 19-year-olds out of work was more than one in four, with the 635,000 on the dole accounting for one-fifth of the total.

Commission predicts in its latest *Labour Market Quarterly Report*.

But there must be doubts over whether the present Youth Opportunities Programme (YOP) or the 'son of YOP' can cope with the enormous numbers involved. In its brief three-year life, it has already trebled in size. In 1978-79 it provided 162,000 places and catered for one in eight school leavers. In 1981-82 it will provide 440,000 places (540,000 places if the MSC has its way) and cater for nearly one in two leavers.[1] The MSC is now having to find almost 10,000 new places a week which will provide worthwhile work experience and useful training – equivalent to creating a firm the size of Hoover every week.

As it is, there have been persistent complaints that many placements provide 'make-work' of little value and no real training; and that unscrupulous employers have exploited the YOP to avoid recruiting permanent staff. There is also the question of what happens to youngsters when they finish their placements, which last an average of six months or so. Some are already coming round for their second YOP spell. In autumn 1979, seven out of ten YOP 'graduates' found jobs afterwards. A few months later, the number was down to six in ten. By the end of 1980, it was fewer than three in ten.[2] But supporters of YOP remain committed and enthusiastic. 'I don't think anyone would have given these youngsters a chance without the Programme', says Mrs Mary Matthews, company secretary of a shopfitting firm near Doncaster, which employs 23 permanent staff and has been taking boys and girls on work experience placements since the YOP started.

Of the other special employment schemes, Community Industry, which is run under the auspices of the National Association of Youth Clubs, also caters for 16- and 17-year-olds in areas of high unemployment or the inner cities. They are paid the going rate for jobs intended to benefit the community like painting and decorating, landscaping and building renovation. The remaining measures, the Temporary Short Time Working Compensation Scheme, the Job Release Scheme and the Community Enterprise Programme (CEP), all aim to help adults, the first two permanently.

1 The number of places available in 1983-84 for the Youth Training Scheme, YOP's successor, was 460,000 and better job opportunities meant that not all of these were being taken up.
2 It has now improved to four in ten for summer 1983 YOP 'graduates'.

The CEP projects cover a wide range. In Skelmersdale, the CEP supports cooperative industry with training workshops. One company repairs and renovates school furniture and another makes metal pallets and containers. Harlow Council has nineteen people on projects at present – everything from clearing estates of rubbish and working on archaeological finds. And it has put in for projects ranging from boatbuilding and renovation to care for the elderly and mobile theatre.

Compared with the resources available for young people, however, unemployed adults get a pretty raw deal, with only a third as much being spent on the CEP as on the YOP. Yet the MSC estimates that by the beginning of 1983 nearly a million people will have been out of work for more than a year, close to one in three of the unemployed total, compared with under one in five in January 1981. And the number of long-term unemployed will go on rising for some time after the total starts to level off.[1]

The Job Release scheme – under which workers nearing retirement get a weekly allowance if they make way for someone on the dole – has had relatively little impact, mainly because workers do not want to or cannot afford to retire early. And the short-time compensation scheme, which is due to be run down, has mostly been used by employers, particularly in manufacturing such as textiles and engineering, who felt their problems were temporary. With the recession stretching out into the future there must be anxieties over redundancies which will follow removal of the subsidy.

Similar criticisms to those of YOP are directed at schemes to help adults: that the projects chosen are often of little value; that firms get subsidies for workers they would have taken on anyway, or that permanent recruitment is inhibited; and that firms may even get an unfair advantage as a result, displacing workers in competitor firms who lose business.

It is a criticism of all special programmes that the spending is merely a form of back-door reflation, and the money would be better spent on conventional reflation measures such as tax cuts. But the MSC stoutly maintains that special programmes, apart

---

1 In October 1983, 1.15 million people had been out of work for more than a year – 37 per cent of all those unemployed. The number would have been higher without measures enabling older men to declare themselves retired rather than unemployed and the switch to a computerised count of benefit recipients from registration at job centres.

from directing help at the most vulnerable groups, ensure that the maximum number of jobs are created for the cash available, avoiding dissipation into imports or capital intensive projects. The difficulty is that most of these jobs are only temporary.

If the government continues to insist that it cannot expand the economy and hence start bringing unemployment down, special programmes are the only weapon at its disposal. It ought to remember, though, that unemployment does not stop hurting when youngsters come of age.

*   *   *

When Mrs Thatcher announced the new measures to cut youth unemployment in July 1981, she included a scheme designed to have a fundamental impact on the workings of the labour market. The scheme, reputedly the brainchild of Professor Alan Walters, the Prime Minister's special economic adviser, will pay employers a £15-a-week subsidy for youngsters aged under 18 employed in their first year of leaving school, provided they are paid less than £40 a week.[1]

This scheme takes as its starting point the belief that youth unemployment is higher than it need be because wages paid to inexperienced young people are too high in relation to adult earnings. By giving employers a financial incentive to pay youngsters less than £40 a week, substantially below the present pay rates in most jobs, the government is acting to force down market wage rates for young people. It hopes that more jobs for youngsters will be created as a result, both directly in the subsidised firms and as a consequence of the spillover effects on the pay of young people in general.

The Walters scheme, as it was undoubtedly intended to, poses particular difficulties for the 27 statutory Wages Councils, covering three million workers in poorly unionised occupations such as catering and retailing, which fix minimum wage rates. The four largest Councils, covering two million workers, all set rates of more than £40 a week to 17-year-olds and two of them set rates of more than £40 to 16-year-olds. Employers paying less than this are liable for prosecution and will obviously not be able to take advantage of the subsidy scheme.

Mrs Thatcher said in Parliament that she hoped the Wages

1 As at November 1983 the maximum wage for a £15 a week subsidy was £42 and for a £7.50 subsidy was £47.

The Government's Special Employment and Training Measures

	Numbers covered May 1981	Numbers covered Sept. 1983	Cost 1983-84 £million
1. Community Industry	6,500	8,000	25
2. Community Programme	14,500	97,000	388
3. Enterprise Allowance	n.a.	7,894	28
4. Job Release Scheme	54,800	85,000	304
5. Job Splitting Scheme	n.a.	610	29
6. Temporary Short Time Working Compensation Scheme	687,600	36,000	34
7. Adult training	28,900	3,000	276
8. Young Workers Scheme	n.a.	102,000	75
9. Youth Opportunities Programme	155,000	75,000 }	
10. Youth Training Scheme	n.a.	198,000 }	904
	947,300	612,504	2,082*

*Including £7m for the voluntary projects programme, which funds the administration costs of employing jobless workers to do voluntary work, and £12m for careers service strengthening.

1. Run under the auspices of the National Association of Youth Clubs and provides temporary jobs on socially worthwhile projects for disadvantaged young people aged 16 to 19.

2. Provides temporary employment for long-term unemployed adults on community projects. Replaces Community Enterprise Programme.

3. Pays allowance to unemployed people who want to start their own business, who lose entitlement to social security benefits.

4. Provides weekly allowance for workers approaching retirement age to make way for someone on the dole.

5. Pays grant to employer who splits an existing full-time job into two part-time ones.

6. Subsidises short-time working as an alternative to redundancies.

7. Subsidises training opportunities in industry.

8. Pays subsidy to employers who take on school leavers at £47 a week or less.

9. Provides training and work experience for up to a year for under-18s.

10. Provides 'high quality integrated' programme of training and planned work experience lasting up to a year, 'designed to give school leavers a range of practical transferable skills to enable them to compete more effectively in the labour market.'

Source: Department of Employment

Councils, independent bodies comprising representatives from employers, trade unions and independents, 'will take into account the measures we proposed'. Union opposition to pay rate cuts for youngsters in work is likely to impose a check on the subsidy scheme's effectiveness. But even without such opposition its success must be in doubt.

In an unpublished review of special employment programmes, the MSC points out that two previous subsidy programmes, the Small Firms Employment Subsidy and the Youth Employment Subsidy, had to be abandoned because it was found that most of the people being subsidised – three out of four in the case of YES – would have been employed anyway or were being employed only at the expense of others, for example adults on full pay.

The government admits that the new scheme will subsidise youngsters who already have jobs, and that there is a risk that older workers will be displaced by the attractions of cheaper young alternatives. But the Department of Employment reckons that the scheme could take perhaps 15,000 to 20,000 school leavers permanently off the register by March 1983 when it is fully operational, and ministers believe that by reducing wage costs it will lead to the long-term creation of new permanent jobs.

In September 1983 the Walters scheme, called the Young Workers Scheme, was subsidising 102,000 youngsters in work after peaking at 130,000 the previous March. The decline may reflect the impact of the Youth Training Scheme. The Young Workers Scheme has undoubtedly proved expensive: an official study released early in 1983 estimated that it was costing the government £5,355 for every new job created. Less than a quarter of the jobs subsidised would not have existed otherwise – a record as bad if not worse than the Youth Employment Subsidy.

IV Productivity, Competitiveness and Investment

Introduction

The rapid growth of manufacturing productivity since 1980 has provided Mrs Thatcher's government with one of its main claims to success. Between winter 1980 and the third quarter of 1983 output per person employed in manufacturing climbed by 20 per cent, compared with a rise in output of only 2 per cent, a far bigger increase than could have been predicted on the basis of past experience. Productivity gains were widespread throughout industry, though motor vehicles, steel and engineering stand out.

In the past, productivity has tended to follow closely changes in output. When output falls productivity falls, because companies do not respond immediately to a drop in demand by laying off workers. If the decline in demand continues, lay-offs may follow, but companies have traditionally kept on workers in downswings to be sure of having enough skilled labour when demand picks up once more.

When output starts to rise the process happens in reverse. At first factories boost production by increasing overtime working for existing employees, ending short-time and so on. This produces a sharp increase in output per head. Later, however, firms take on more workers to cope with the extra demand, tempering the productivity gains made earlier. The result is that productivity rises sharply in the early stages of a cyclical recovery before flattening out, and falls quite steeply in the downturn.

In the latest recession, however, the pattern has been rather different. Productivity did indeed fall as output slumped in late 1979 and 1980, but by less than might have been predicted. And from the winter of 1980, when output was still falling, it began to

OUTPUT AND PRODUCTIVITY
Seasonally adjusted 1980 = 100

WHOLE ECONOMY
— Output per person employed
······ Output

MANUFACTURING
— Output per person hour
— Output per person employed
······ Output

Source: Department of Employment Gazette

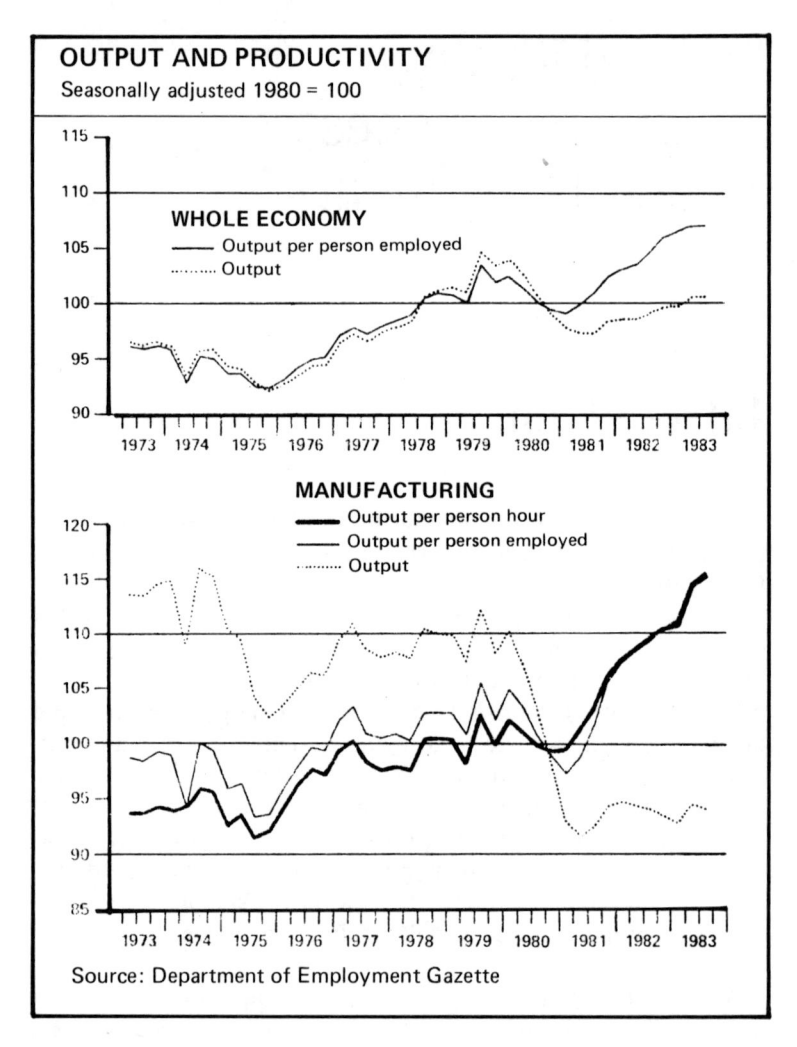

rise sharply and has continued to do so despite the most tentative of industrial recoveries. During 1981, output per head jumped by more than 10 per cent. This slowed to 3.5 per cent during 1982 when manufacturing production fell slightly, only to revive again in 1983. In the year to autumn 1983, productivity rose by over 6 per cent.

In the post-1979 recession the shake-out of labour was bigger and faster than the drop in output. By late 1983, with jobs still being shed though at a slower pace, employment in manufacturing had fallen by a quarter from pre-recession levels, while output was down by one-sixth. The government's explanation of these events might run as follows. The extent of labour shedding shows how serious wasteful staffing was in British industry before the Conservatives took over. But the recession, though regrettably severe, has made industry 'leaner and fitter' by eliminating over-manning, weeding out the most inefficient companies and speeding up the transfer of resources to new high-productivity uses. It should now be better equipped to meet foreign competition and preserve jobs.

'Supply side' policies of trade union reform, privatisation of state-owned industries and lower tax rates for top managers have encouraged improvements in efficiency, on this view. So has the government's insistence that it will not bail industry out of its difficulties by subsidies or through reflation of the economy. Ministers are constantly hearing from industrialists of a changed attitude on the shop floor, of improved working practices, increased flexibility and an end to demarcation arguments. These signify permanent productivity gains and pave the way for more.

Other economists have been more sceptical of the so-called 'productivity miracle'. If companies, realising that the recession was likely to be prolonged, decide not to hoard labour any longer this is not in itself a sign of greater efficiency, they argue. It does not mean that those left are more productive than before. Similarly, the widespread scrapping of less efficient plant and machinery, and the closure of factories, has raised the average productivity of the remainder on an arithmetic basis. But that does not necessarily represent an underlying productivity improvement. It is a once-for-all gain which does not alter the basic trend.

The recent spurt in productivity can be almost wholly explained by the normal cyclical improvement and the scrapping of inefficient capacity, some economists have suggested. As Professors Buiter and Miller have put it:

'In short, the current productivity record of much of British industry is like the cricket team that improves its batting average by only playing its better batsmen! As long as the tail-enders score some runs, however, it would surely be better to play them even if it does lower the side's batting average.'[1]

[1] Willem Buiter and Marcus Miller, 'The Macro-economic Consequences of a Change in Regime: The UK Under Mrs Thatcher', Paper to Brookings Panel on Economic Activity, September 1983.

The sceptics say that in the long run, productivity cannot be put on a higher trend without investment in new and more efficient machinery. But the recession has slashed manufacturing investment by a third. They are also worried that when the economy revives, some or all of the gains already made will be eroded. For instance, trade unions may try to reassert their influence when their bargaining position is stronger. The 'evidence of a new attitude on the shop floor' may not survive recovery. Lack of cooperation between management and workers, and the poor quality of much of British management, may yet inhibit productivity growth, they say.

In 1983, the economy was still operating too far below capacity to judge which side has the best of the argument. But it is worth noting that between 1966 and 1973, before the first oil price shock, output per head rose by 3.2 per cent a year in the economy as a whole and by 4.4 per cent in manufacturing. Between 1973 and 1979 productivity growth slowed to about 1.5 per cent a year. Doubling the trend productivity growth would get Britain back on its pre-OPEC path. To do much better would be unprecedented.

Improved productivity brings with it many benefits. Other things being equal, it will boost economic growth, raise living standards and reduce inflation. But unless total output in the economy rises as fast as productivity, unemployment will increase. In the past, economic growth and higher productivity have gone hand in hand. Each helps to generate the other. Growth, by raising output and encouraging investment, increases productivity. Greater productivity, by expanding the productive potential of the economy, spurs output. But two new factors have come into play.

One is the advent of new technology – the micro-processor revolution – which is capable of transforming working methods not only in industry but also in the service sector which has provided most of the extra jobs in the past decade or so. The fear of many is that the economy will not be able to absorb the huge number of workers who may be displaced. So far, however, the spread of the new technology has been gradual. There is no sign that the recent productivity gains stem from the introduction of micro-processors. And the doom-mongers tend to forget that novel technologies generate new activities and industries which employ many people – computer software, video libraries, computer games and, to come, cable television, to name just a few.

But the second factor is the reluctance of governments to let demand in the economy expand rapidly for fear of reviving inflation. There is then a danger that productivity growth will persistently outstrip economic output and unemployment will go on rising. Simulations on models of the economy all tend to suggest that a big improvement in productivity will create more jobless because demand will not keep pace.

The threat to jobs is not, however, a good reason for opposing moves to improve efficiency. The answer must be to try to ensure that the economy grows fast enough to absorb as many of the displaced workers as possible in other activities – and to see that the benefits of higher living standards are spread more evenly between those who are still working and those who are not.

Productivity is one of the key influences on Britain's competitiveness in international markets and hence on output and jobs at home. High wage increases and a poor productivity record consistently worsened competitiveness throughout the 1970s, and this was exacerbated in the second half of the decade by the strengthening pound. The 50 per cent loss of competitiveness between early 1979 and the beginning of 1981, the result of the 1979 pay explosion and a 25 per cent appreciation of sterling, proved devastating for industry. By late 1983, lower wage increases and rising productivity had slowed the growth of unit labour costs. But even with a substantial drop in the value of the pound, only half that loss of competitiveness had been recouped.

The battle to improve competitiveness has not been helped by developments abroad. Britain can only better her position without recourse to devaluation if unit labour costs rise more slowly than those of her international rivals. But economic recovery means that productivity, which was dampened by recession, has begun to improve in most countries. Even if it only gets back on trend – and it should do better than that in the early stages of the upswing – this would mean productivity growth of 2.5 per cent in the United States, 3 per cent in West Germany, 4 per cent in France and 4.5 per cent in Japan.

In the year to mid-1983, wage costs per unit of output grew by 3.4 per cent in Britain. But in the United States and Japan they grew by only 2 per cent, and in Germany unit wage costs did not rise at all over the year. All this serves to demonstrate how fast Britain has to run to stand still in the international race for competitiveness. Furthermore, the modest increase in wage costs in Britain owed more to the rapid rise in output per head than to

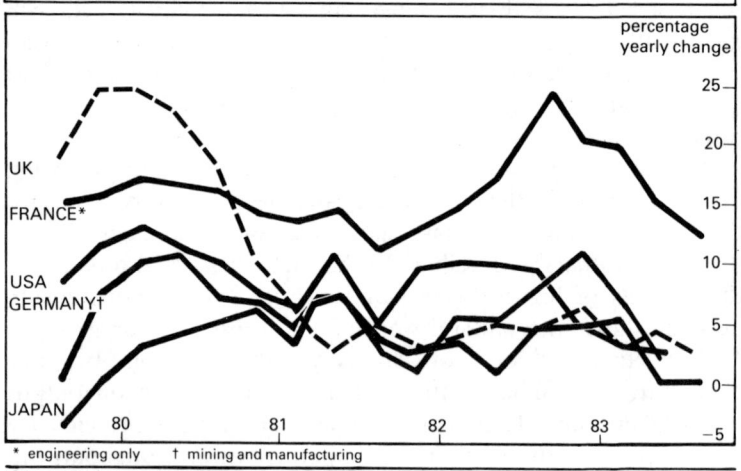

WAGE COSTS PER UNIT OF OUTPUT IN MANUFACTURING INDUSTRY

* engineering only   † mining and manufacturing

Sources: National Institute of Economic and Social Research;
Organisation for Economic Cooperation & Development;
Department of Employment

lower pay deals, which remain well above those in successful competitor countries. The danger persists that when productivity growth fades, unit wage costs will shoot up once more.

There would seem to be no alternative to some further depreciation of sterling if British goods are to be priced back into world markets. This does not mean, however, that containing unit labour costs is unimportant. It reduces the need for devaluation, which cuts real incomes and puts up inflation. But the government would be unwise to pretend to British workers that the achievement of greater competitiveness lies in their hands alone. That could prove a recipe for certain disappointment.

One factor behind the surge in the pound between 1979 and 1981 – apart from Britain's new-found oil wealth – was the high level of UK interest rates, which had a direct impact on industry's costs. Each 1 per cent rise in bank base lending rates – to which overdraft and other loan rates are tied – costs industry about £250m a year. The cash squeeze which followed the jump in base lending rates from 12 to 17 per cent forced companies to slash stocks, sack workers and chop back investment just to keep their heads above water. Many still went under.

It is sometimes argued that what matters to industry is the

level of real interest rates – adjusted for inflation – rather than nominal rates. Real rates are clearly important. If the cost of borrowing is far greater than, say, the likely rise in the value of a company's stocks, it will be reluctant to finance the rebuilding of stocks on credit. Conversely, when, in periods of rapid inflation, interest rates tend to lag behind so that real rates are negative, companies have an incentive to borrow to restock.

But nominal rates are crucial. The reason is what is known in the jargon as 'frontloading'. Suppose inflation is 10 per cent and the nominal interest rate is 12 per cent – a real rate of 2 per cent. The lender gets 10 per cent of the sum he has lent each year to compensate him for the fact that inflation will have reduced the value of the original sum by the time it comes to be repaid. From the borrower's point of view, however, this inflation premium is in effect an early repayment of the loan. The higher the inflation premium, the greater the burden that early repayment puts on the borrower. It matters a good deal to industry whether a 2 per cent real rate of interest is accompanied by inflation of zero, 10 or 20 per cent.

There is also much argument over how to measure the real rate of interest. Most people agree that it should reflect expected inflation rather than past or present rates – but how are expected rates to be measured? One way is to look at the yield on conventional gilt-edged stocks compared with index-linked stocks. Another is to take the predictions of economic forecasting groups.

Which inflation rate is relevant – should it be retail prices, producer prices or the GDP deflator – the broadest measure of inflation in the economy? Should interest rates be measured before or after tax relief? Depending on the answers given to all these questions, real interest rates in summer 1983 may have been as low as minus 2 per cent or as high as plus 10.5 per cent.[1]

Abstracting from all these difficulties, some broad idea of trends in real rates can be got from comparing bank base rates with past inflation. On this basis, real rates have typically averaged about 2.5 per cent, though for a large part of the 1970s – a period of rapid inflation – they were strongly negative. In the last year or so they have averaged 3 to 4 per cent.

The level of interest rates has a significant impact on the

1 See 'Can interest rates fall?', *Lloyds Bank Economic Bulletin*, No. 55, July 1983.

economy through its effect on company cash flow, stockbuilding and investment, though the precise way it works is still not clear. High interest rates have not, however, been to blame for Britain's comparatively low rate of investment in earlier years. The main problem seems to have been the very low returns available on investment projects. Over the past 20 years, rates of return on fixed capital in Britain have averaged less than half those in the United States and Japan.

In manufacturing the comparisons are even more dismal. In 1981 the rate of return on capital had sunk to 3 per cent in Britain (from 8 per cent in 1978) compared with 14 per cent in Canada, 12 per cent in the United States (down from 21 per cent three years earlier) and 14 per cent in Germany in 1981. Manufacturing investment, after rising by about 20 per cent between 1972 and 1979, slumped by a third as the recession set in, which was only partly offset by higher investment in services and distribution. In addition, investment by the public sector in Britain has fallen sharply over the past decade. Between 1972 and 1982, fixed capital formation by central and local government fell by 60 per cent (part of which was due to council house sales which count as negative investment spending). As a proportion of total investment, general government spending shrank from a quarter to a tenth.

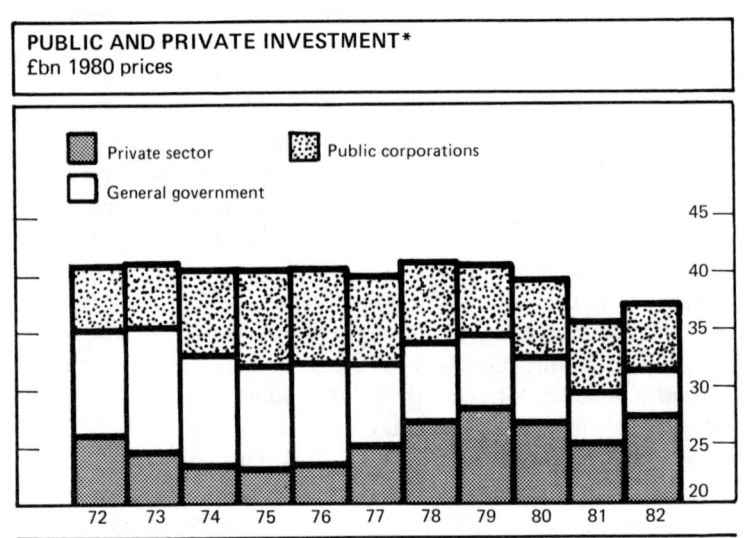

PUBLIC AND PRIVATE INVESTMENT*
£bn 1980 prices

- Private sector
- Public corporations
- General government

*Gross domestic fixed capital formation, all industries and services, including dwellings.
Source: *National Income and Expenditure 1983*, Blue Book

The first piece in this section, 'The cost of higher productivity', discusses the implications of a higher rate of productivity growth for unemployment. 'Industry needs more than lower interest rates' analyses why the government is pinning its faith on lower rates to revive the economy. And 'Sterling's slide is good news for industry', which was written as the pound began to fall in November 1982, explains why this was welcomed by industry but aroused mixed feelings in government.

1 The cost of higher productivity

Published October 20 1982

If Britain were to produce her present economic output with a productivity performance equal to that of Germany, 7.5 million jobs would disappear tomorrow. If British workers produced the same output per head as their American counterparts, 9.5 million jobs would go. These startling figures are a measure both of Britain's dismal productivity record in recent years and of the painful dilemma confronting government in any attempt to improve economic performance.

The more rapidly productivity increases the more jobs are lost for any given economic output. But the slower productivity rises the slower the growth of economic output and living standards, the greater the inflationary pressures (because demands for better living standards cannot be satisfied), the smaller the incentives to invest and the less well equipped firms are to meet foreign competition. This means job losses now and worse employment prospects in the future. Had Britain kept pace with Germany, instead of falling further and further behind, we would probably, like them, be about 50 per cent better off and our industries would have been in far better shape to withstand the recession. Fewer jobs might then have disappeared.

As the National Institute of Economic and Social Research reveals in its August 1982 *Review*, Britain is less efficient at producing things than any of its main international rivals in Europe, the United States or Japan. It lags behind the others in practically every sector of the economy except farming. In

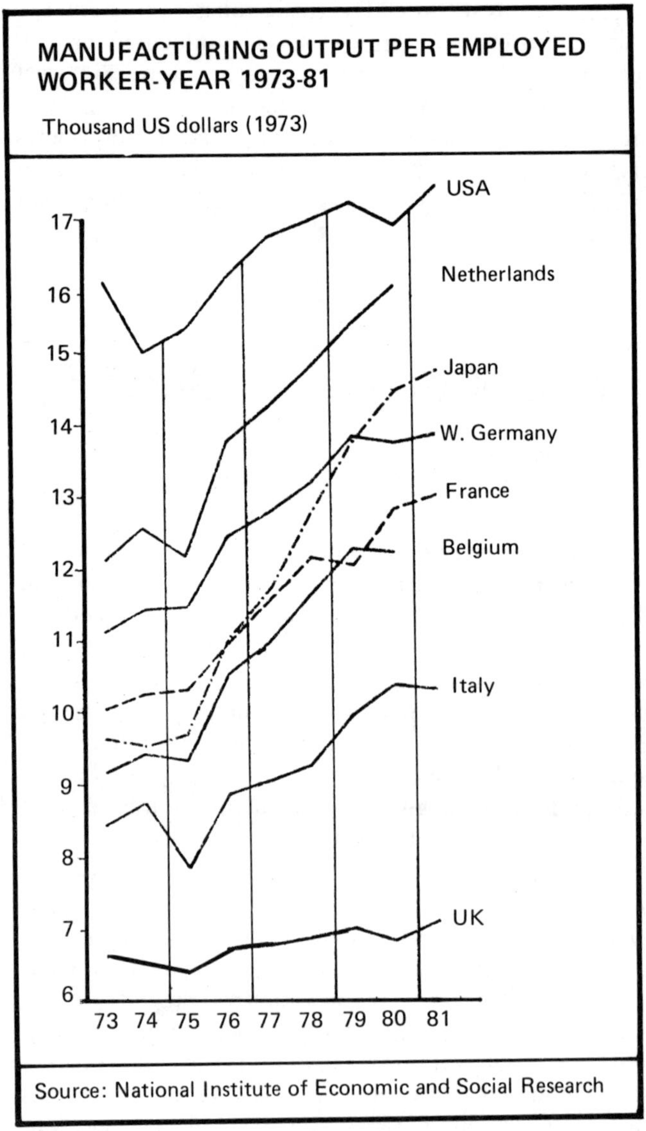
MANUFACTURING OUTPUT PER EMPLOYED WORKER-YEAR 1973-81
Thousand US dollars (1973)
USA
Netherlands
Japan
W. Germany
France
Belgium
Italy
UK
17
16
15
14
13
12
11
10
9
8
7
6
73 74 75 76 77 78 79 80 81
Source: National Institute of Economic and Social Research

1980, output per head in Germany was about 50 per cent higher than in Britain, in the United States about 66 per cent higher and in Japan 12 per cent higher. The bulk of this disparity results from Britain's abysmal performance in manufacturing. In 1980, manufacturing output per head in Germany and Japan was more than twice as high as in Britain. In the United States it was 2.5 times as high.

Even though manufacturing now accounts for only a quarter of total activity in this country, it remains the most potent determinant of economic growth and the single most important factor dragging Britain down the international league table. It is also the sector most exposed to foreign competition – with the result that poor competitiveness leads directly to a worsening trade balance and falling employment.

Britain lost her pre-eminent position as the workshop of the world to America a century ago. But Germany did not move decisively ahead until the late 1950s and Japan only in the 1970s. Since 1973, however, when the first oil price shock brought an era of strong world growth abruptly to an end, the gap between Britain and her rivals has widened into a chasm. Between 1973 and 1980, output per head in British manufacturing increased by just 6 per cent. In Canada and the United States it rose 20 per cent, in Germany and Italy by 25 per cent, in France by 30 per cent and in Japan by 40 per cent. The leap in British productivity over the past 18 months or so – up by 12 per cent in manufacturing between the end of 1980 and mid-1982 – makes little difference to the overall picture. As the National Institute points out, another 50 per cent, if not more, would still be necessary to bring us to European levels.

The reasons for slow productivity growth in this country are complex. It is not simply a question of the amount of investment or the introduction of new technologies. Indeed, British industry has maintained a relatively high level of investment in recent years, though mostly to economise on expensive labour and energy. But a lot of investment needs changes in manning and organisation at work if it is to bring significant productivity gains and it is here that some of the serious problems have arisen. Firms simply have not been able to persuade workers to accept job reductions or flexible manning arrangements, especially in the last ten years or so when they may not have been able to offer alternative jobs and employment opportunities elsewhere have been dwindling. It is only during the present recession that firms have been able to force through new working practices and job losses because the alternatives such as closure were clearly much worse. Even so, in a survey of 50 large firms employing nearly 700,000 people by the National Institute in late 1981, more than half said their manning was still excessive and the same proportion claimed they could increase their output by at least 10 per cent without taking on more workers.

The experience of the past eighteen months has raised hopes that Britain may now be set on a path of more rapid productivity growth. It is not yet clear, however, to what extent recent gains have been due simply to shutting down or mothballing less productive capacity which cannot be repeated. And there is a limit to the extent to which productivity can be improved by shedding workers. At some point there has to be new investment – and this is unlikely to take place while demand and so profitability remain depressed and existing capacity is underused. Slow economic growth can thus be a cause as well as the consequence of sluggish productivity growth.

What would the effect on jobs be if productivity continued to rise rapidly in future? Since the same output will be produced more efficiently, jobs will be shed. But higher productivity will also tend to boost output. If the benefit comes through in lower prices (calculators, computers), consumers will have more spending power to spend on these and other things. Higher pay for the workers concerned will do the same. And if the gains are translated into higher profits, these can be ploughed back into investment, providing jobs in capital goods industries and expanding capacity to provide jobs in the future.

Higher productivity also helps improve international competitiveness by curbing the rise in unit labour costs. The employment impact of this can be substantial. According to the Confederation of British Industry every 1 per cent loss of world trade in manufacturing costs 250,000 jobs. Every 1 per cent of the home market lost to imports costs 80,000 jobs.

Even with these benefits, however, strong productivity growth means unemployment will climb. Economic output would need to grow by at least 3 per cent a year for 10 years – double the rate during most of the 1970s – to raise output per head to *present* West German levels without unemployment rising further. Few forecasters believe that is likely.

The Economist Intelligence Unit, which recently ran a high productivity scenario through the Treasury's model of the economy, found that doubling the growth of output per head led to national output in 1985 being rather higher and inflation substantially lower than otherwise. But employment dropped by nearly 700,000, equivalent to more than 500,000 extra people on the dole.

The government is thus faced with two imperatives. It must try to provide the conditions under which the economy can grow as rapidly as possible without overheating, to facilitate productivity growth and help absorb the workers whose jobs are lost into other occupations. But it must also try to ensure that the benefits of change are not unfairly hogged by those lucky enough to remain in work. And that may mean, among other things, shorter working hours and so on to spread work more thinly, investment for training in new skills, job creation in labour-intensive socially desirable activities such as environmental improvement and welfare services, and a fairer distribution of income between workers and non-workers in the future.

2 Industry needs more than lower interest rates

Published August 18 1982

On August 18 the clearing banks cut their base lending rates by 0.5 percentage points to 11 per cent, the third reduction in little over a month, as the government nudged interest rates down to help industry pull out of recession.

The Chancellor of the Exchequer, Sir Geoffrey Howe, is pinning his hopes for industrial recovery firmly on the government's policy of gradually reducing interest rates – the cornerstone of his budget strategy this year. Yet the evidence that interest rates have a powerful influence on economic activity is less than overwhelming. The economics textbooks say that a cut in interest rates boosts investment by cheapening the cost of borrowing so that projects which were previously unprofitable become worthwhile. But surveys by the Confederation of British Industry show that the cost of funds is a relatively unimportant deterrent to investment. Most capital spending is financed from retained profits – though the proportion has fallen from 73 per cent in

1977 to 61 per cent in 1981[1] – and decisions on whether to go ahead with projects depend critically on the outlook for demand and profitability.

The Treasury's more sophisticated theory, now enshrined in its model of the economy, is that lower interest rates boost investment by increasing the amount of cash available for it. Just as lower inflation, by boosting the purchasing power of people's incomes, tends to increase demand, so a cut in interest rates, by reducing borrowing costs and improving cash flow, will tend to encourage investment. Every 1 per cent fall in bank base lending rates puts £250 million into industry's coffers, with the full impact feeding through after about six months. 'It is a simple fact of life', Sir Terence Beckett, CBI Director-General, said recently, 'that lower interest rates lead to greater profitability, more investment and more jobs.'

Yet having the cash available is no guarantee that it will be spent on investment, as the famous cash mountain of GEC so clearly demonstrates. With factories, machines and workers still idle, and the economic outlook uncertain, there is little incentive to add to capacity. Industry could produce plenty more with the plant and machinery it already has. And even replacement investment to improve efficiency and cut costs, which has been relatively buoyant during the recession, can seem pretty pointless if further cutbacks in capacity are threatened, as British Steel is finding. In these circumstances it is not surprising that many companies have taken advantage of cheaper borrowing to build up liquidity instead. Corporate cash assets are now higher in real terms than at any time in the past seven years.

The one key exception is house building which is highly sensitive to interest rate changes, mainly because of the impact these have on mortgage costs and so people's demand for homes to buy. House building was one of the most dynamic sectors pulling the economy out of the 1930s depression, and it has powerful spillover effects elsewhere in the economy, providing jobs not only in construction, but also in related industries such as home improvements, furniture, carpets and so on.

Stock-building too tends to be more sensitive than fixed investment to the level of interest rates. The hikes in rates by the present government in 1979 in its bid to curb money growth imposed a cash squeeze which was one of the chief causes of the

1 60 per cent in 1982.

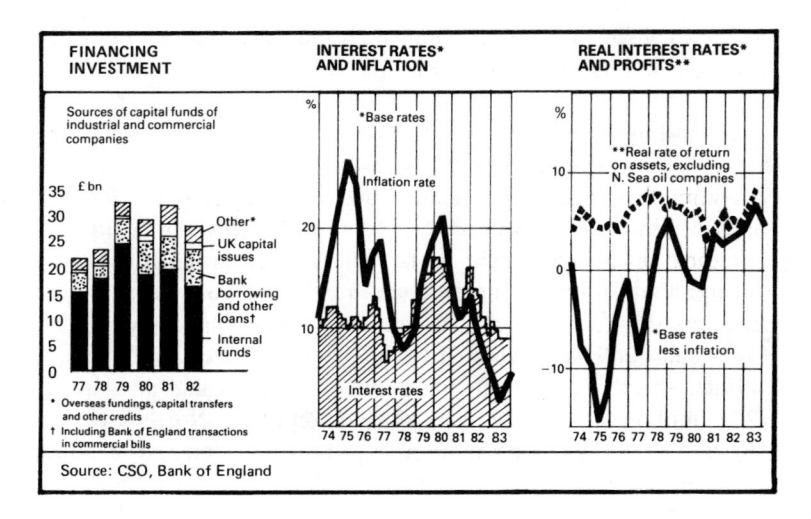

Productivity, Competitiveness and Investment

FINANCING INVESTMENT — Sources of capital funds of industrial and commercial companies (£ bn, 77–82): Other*, UK capital issues, Bank borrowing and other loans†, Internal funds.
* Overseas fundings, capital transfers and other credits
† Including Bank of England transactions in commercial bills

INTEREST RATES* AND INFLATION (74–83): *Base rates, Inflation rate, Interest rates

REAL INTEREST RATES* AND PROFITS* (74–83): **Real rate of return on assets, excluding N. Sea oil companies; *Base rates less inflation

Source: CSO, Bank of England

huge rundown in stocks which precipitated the recession. The government is now relying on rebuilding of those stocks to stoke the fires of economic recovery. But, as the summer 1982 issue of the *Midland Bank Review* points out, greater uncertainty about future demand, better stock control and changes in the tax rules which no longer favour stock-building could well combine to keep stock levels down, irrespective of interest rates.

On the other hand, lower interest rates undoubtedly improve business confidence in the economic outlook, and this in itself may be an important stimulus to restocking and investment. It certainly works the other way. As ministers and Whitehall officials ruefully admit, the four-point jump in rates in autumn 1981 following a sterling scare and booming bank lending was a disastrous blow to confidence which abruptly cut short the beginnings of industrial revival from the trough of recession that spring. Indeed, one reason why the authorities have been so cautious about cutting interest rates again this time is that they do not want to risk having to put them up again later.

When it comes to the personal sector, the impact of lower interest rates is decidedly ambiguous. On paper, the personal sector benefits more from higher interest on its savings in building societies and banks than it does from lower interest payments on mortgages and loans. On the other hand, hard-pressed families with mortgages are more likely to spend the extra income released by lower payments than savers, principally the elderly, are to cut back when their interest income falls. Of course a drop in interest rates would also swell consumer spending if people decided to save less or borrow more as a result. But people have already built up debt to near-record levels and are unlikely to want to increase it further. Savings too have held up despite cuts in interest rates over the past year.[1]

By far the most crucial economic benefit from lower interest rates is, however, their impact on competitiveness, partly through a reduction in industry's costs, but much more importantly through their effect on the exchange rate. The CBI wants interest rates cut by enough to push sterling down, especially against European currencies where Britain's chief export markets lie.

Each 1 per cent drop in the pound's overall value adds about £200 million to company profits (excluding North Sea oil operations) by widening margins and boosting demand at home and abroad. But for this to happen the government must cut interest rates faster than they are falling elsewhere, notably in the United States, which it has been reluctant to do. The pound's overall value is as high now as it was at the beginning of the year when base rates were 3.5 per cent above today's levels. Worse, it is weaker against the dollar and stronger against European currencies, exacerbating the competitiveness problem rather than easing it.

The government is frightened to let interest rates fall too far for fear a gentle sterling slide, which they would accept, should turn into a rout, jeopardising their hopes on inflation by pushing up import costs and relaxing the pressure on companies to keep costs down. And they are also worried that too sharp a fall might put their monetary targets at risk, by encouraging bank lending.

But the government's caution has meant that although nominal interest rates have come down slowly, real interest rates – adjusted for inflation – have gone up. Unless rates come down more quickly than inflation, the real burden of borrowing costs will not lessen. Blue chip borrowers who can get overdrafts at 1 per cent over base rate will from today be paying more than 3 per cent over the present rate of inflation and 4.5 per cent more than the 7.5 per cent inflation rate officially predicted by Christmas, which is perhaps more relevant.[2] These are high real rates by

1 In fact, the personal sector went on borrowing heavily through 1983 and saved less, largely because low inflation reduced the amount of saving needed to maintain the real value of financial assets. The savings ratio halved from 16 per cent in late 1980 to 8 per cent in summer 1983.
2 The actual figure for December 1982 was 5.4 per cent.

historical standards, especially for an economy still in deep recession. Companies are not going to invest in stocks financed by borrowing at 12 per cent when those stocks are unlikely to rise in value by more than 7.5 per cent.

Yesterday's base rate cut to 11 per cent leaves nominal interest rates only 1 per cent lower than a year ago, and real interest rates rather higher. This is hardly likely to promote the sort of stimulus which would get the Chancellor off the hook this autumn. The chief virtue of lower rates is to help make expansion possible – but they will not make it happen on their own.

The cuts in interest rates over the course of 1982 – from 14 per cent in January to 9 per cent in November – did help to revive economic activity but this was almost entirely by way of higher consumer spending after two reductions in the mortgage rate, helped along by an increase in housebuilding. The growth in total investment slowed in the second half of 1982 and the first half of 1983, while stocks fell sharply in the autumn and winter of 1982 and were rebuilt only modestly in the following six months.

In November 1982 interest rates went up again, first to 10 per cent and then, in January, to 11 per cent as sterling weakened. By March 1983 they were once more on their way down and in October 1983 were reduced to 9 per cent, where they had been a year earlier. Inflation was a little lower than in 1982, around 5 per cent instead of 6 per cent in the fourth quarter. Real interest rates were thus a percentage point or so higher.

3 Sterling's slide is good news for industry

Published November 17 1982

In November 1982 the British economy still looked sickly, even though the low point of the recession had been reached 18 months before. The high value of sterling attracted much of the blame. In the four months between July and early November 1982 the authorities cut bank base lending rates from 12 to 9 per cent to ease the pressure on industry and, without saying so explicitly, made it clear that some fall in the pound, especially against European currencies and the yen, would not be unwelcome. The week before this article was published the Treasury released its autumn economic forecast which showed a zero balance of payments in 1983 after a £5,400m surplus in 1982.

The pound's sudden slide at the start of this week will be welcomed by much of British industry if it marks the beginning of a move towards a more realistic value for sterling. For the past twelve months or so the pound has shown remarkable overall stability in a world of sharply gyrating exchange rates, its effective rate index fluctuating within the narrow band of 90 to 92. This contrasts with earlier years when it soared by more than 25 per cent during 1979 and 1980, only to drop sharply by 12 per cent in 1981.

But sterling's recent stability has not pleased British manufacturers who desperately need a lower pound if they are to regain a significant part of the competitiveness lost in recent years. Between the end of 1978 and early 1981, British competitiveness slumped by more than 50 per cent as the strong pound and the impact of the 1979 pay explosion pushed up labour costs. Of this, only 10 to 15 per cent was regained last year, mostly through the falling pound. This year, competitiveness has actually worsened slightly, despite lower pay settlements and rapid productivity growth, because sterling has been stable and other countries have brought down costs as fast or faster than we have. To claw back a

WHAT HAS HAPPENED TO COMPETITIVENESS*

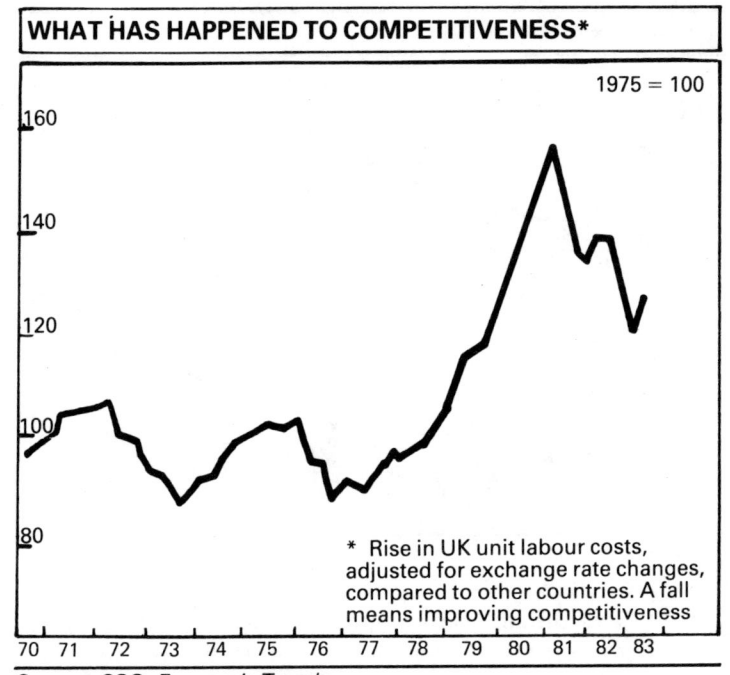

1975 = 100

* Rise in UK unit labour costs, adjusted for exchange rate changes, compared to other countries. A fall means improving competitiveness

Source: CSO, *Economic Trends*

significant part of the competitiveness lost since the mid-1970s solely by its own efforts would take industry many years, to the continuing detriment of output and jobs.

Two-thirds of exporters questioned in the latest Confederation of British Industry industrial trends survey said prices were an important constraint on their ability to export. The Treasury's autumn forecast published last week, which assumes the pound staying around its present levels, predicts a massive deterioration in Britain's balance of trade with exports stagnating and imports the chief beneficiaries of the growth in consumer demand.

Industry's problems have been exacerbated by the marked disparity in the pound's behaviour against different currencies. Sterling is actually not far off its all-time low of $1.55 against the dollar, touched in 1976, having fallen by 15 per cent over the past year and by a third since it peaked in 1980. But it is little lower against the Deutschmark than a year ago and is rather higher against the Japanese yen.

These two currencies are far more important to much of manufacturing industry than the dollar. The dollar is admittedly

STERLING: TAKING THE PLUNGE?

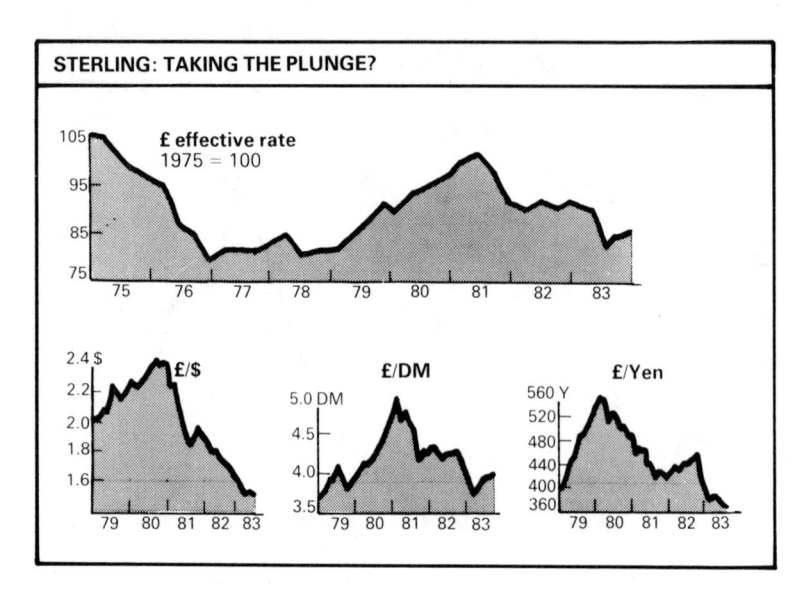

£ effective rate 1975 = 100

£/$ £/DM   £/Yen

the world's and Britain's most important single trading currency. It is used for pricing oil and many raw materials. So dollar movements affect company input costs, at least in the short term (though in the longer run, commodity prices tend to compensate for exchange rate changes). But for most companies even more crucial are the currencies which influence selling prices and profits in principal markets.

The Deutschmark bloc (Germany, the Netherlands and Switzerland, whose currencies tend to move in line) does twice as much trade with Britain in both directions as the United States. Japan, though its total trade with Britain is relatively small, is a leading competitor in some key (and expanding) markets, including consumer and industrial electronics and machine tools.

The pound's surge against all currencies in 1979 and 1980 could be explained by four factors: North Sea oil, possession of which was reckoned to boost sterling by anything from 10 to 20 per cent; a huge balance of payments surplus, due partly to oil and partly to recession; tight money policies which pushed up interest rates to among the highest in Europe; and the so-called 'Thatcher factor' – a feeling of confidence in the government's determination to bring down inflation and set the economy to rights. To a lesser degree these factors helped to buoy the pound this year when the soaring dollar was knocking other currencies for six. This was reinforced by the world banking crisis and the 'flight to quality' which led to substantial overseas buying of government stock.

Now, with oil prices weak, predictions of base rates down to 6 or 7 per cent next year and the forecast elimination of Britain's balance of payments surplus within the next 12 months, not to mention suggestions that the authorities would welcome a lower pound, the markets have looked again and see sterling as ripe for a fall.[1] By contrast, the factors depressing the Deutschmark and the yen in recent months are now evaporating. In Germany, domestic political uncertainties have been largely resolved and the troubles in Poland are less alarming than they were. And the balance of payments, which was plunged into huge deficit by the 1979 oil price shock, has returned to surplus while capital outflows have slowed. In Japan, massive capital outflows, the chief cause of the yen's recent weakness, have virtually come to an end.

The government is unlikely to jack up interest rates to prevent the pound falling, remembering only too well the disastrous impact of last autumn's hikes on business confidence. But it does not want to see a sudden slide, which may mean a pause in the trend to lower interest rates. Apart from being destabilising, ministers are worried that too big a drop will push up import prices and so inflation. This could spark off higher pay claims as workers tried to recoup cuts in real income, eroding the competitiveness gains.

Others argue that the inflation dangers are minimal in a recession of this severity. Importers are likely to take the strain on profit margins rather than putting up prices, while workers are not in a position to win high pay increases. In these circumstances, they say, most of the benefits of a lower pound will feed straight through into output and jobs.

Ministers, one suspects, are in some turmoil. A few months ago, when the decision was made to nudge interest rates down steadily to relieve the pressures on industry and get the economy moving, they were prepared to contemplate some easing of sterling. Now, with their ambitions on inflation so close to

1 In November 1983, bank base rates were 9 per cent, and the latest Treasury forecast put the 1983 balance of payments surplus at £500m, falling to zero in 1984.

coming true, helped along by the strong pound, a sterling slide is the last thing they want.

The pound continued to fall on world currency markets over the next four months, reaching a low point in March when it sank to $1.45, DM3.52 and 346 yen. At bottom its trade-weighted index was 15 per cent below its November level at 78.1.

Bank base lending rates went up twice as interest rates in the money market climbed, first to 10 per cent towards the end of November and then to 11 per cent in January.

Sterling began to pick up in the spring and was fairly steady for the remainder of 1983, its effective rate sticking in the 83 to 85 per cent range. However, with the dollar still gaining ground on the foreign exchanges, sterling was once more weak against the American currency and relatively strong against the Europeans – precisely the combination industry finds least welcome.

The pound's slide over the winter of 1982-83 had remarkably little impact on inflation. Import costs rose quite rapidly, boosted by higher world commodity prices – but the slowdown in unit labour costs, which account for 60 to 70 per cent of industry's total costs, helped companies to absorb the extra and widen profit margins at the same time. Prices charged at the factory gate rose at a steady annual rate of 5.5 per cent or so for most of 1983.

But there was an immediate effect on export prospects. Businesses began to report an upturn in orders as their prices became more attractive to foreign buyers. By the second half of 1983 this optimism had faded, with three-quarters of manufacturing companies surveyed by the Confederation of British Industry complaining that uncompetitive prices were hampering their export trade.

Competitiveness – as measured by the IMF's index of relative unit labour costs adjusted for exchange rate changes – improved by more than 13 per cent between autumn 1982 and early 1983, but worsened again in the summer as the pound rallied.

V The International Scene

Introduction

The rapid growth of world trade in the post-war period has brought about a transformation of the global economy. It has fuelled growth and development in rich and poor nations alike. But in making their economies more open it has also made them more interdependent.

Recession in one country, by cutting imports, hurts the exports and thus the growth prospects of others. Expansion, by boosting import demand, helps other countries to grow. This interdependence through trade has been reinforced by the explosion of international banking, including the Eurodollar market (with more dollars now being held outside than inside the United States), which means that banks throughout the world are deeply involved in other countries' finances, and by the advent of floating exchange rates in 1973.

Huge sums of money can now be moved at the touch of a button from country to country and between currencies. Some $100bn a day is traded on the world's foreign exchange markets, many times what is needed to finance trade. The slightest change in a country's economic or political circumstances can trigger massive movements of capital, aggravating its problems and causing unwelcome repercussions elsewhere.

Exchange rates have not necessarily moved in line with relative competitiveness, or even with changes in the balance of payments, as economic theory would suggest. In recent years, interest rates and, to a lesser extent, political uncertainties have governed financial markets. When exchange rate movements bear little relation to underlying economic performance, they damage not only the economy concerned but others too. Countries with overvalued exchange rates find industry pressing for protection from imports. Protectionist measures, once put in place, are hard to remove even when the exchange rate falls. This breaks the transmission mechanism of world recovery via trade – a very real fear at the present time when developing countries in deep financial trouble are relying on the growth of exports to reduce indebtedness. If they cannot export more they cannot afford to buy more goods from the West. Without their custom the industrial countries risk prolonged economic stagnation.

Countries with undervalued exchange rates, on the other hand, suffer higher inflation and lower living standards, import less and thus act directly as a dampening influence on the world economy. Industry, faced with the possibility of exchange rate changes which overnight can wipe out expectations of future profit, becomes reluctant to invest and take risks. The result is to impair permanently the strength of the world economy.

In 1983, the effects of interdependence have become only too clear. The American economy has experienced a robust recovery accompanied by a huge and widening trade deficit, precisely the conditions which in the past would have been considered ideal to stimulate growth on a global scale. Yet the impact on the rest of the world has been mild. The reason is that the boost from the American trade gap has been offset by the dampening effect of high interest rates and the strong dollar – attributed to record Federal budget deficits. European countries and Japan have felt obliged to keep their interest rates high to protect their currencies and resist importing inflation, while the Third World has found its debt, mostly denominated in dollars, magnified to unmanageable dimensions.

The first oil price shock of 1973-74, which coincided with the final breakdown of the Bretton Woods agreement on fixed exchange rates, was a watershed. The cost of oil quadrupled. Countries plunged into huge balance of payments deficit. Inflation accelerated. Recession began to bite. Into the breach stepped the commercial banking system, lending on the funds deposited with them by the OPEC oil-producers to finance the oil and other imports needed to fuel third world development. This recycling effort appeared to be enormously successful. Growth in developing countries barely hiccuped while the industrial nations stagnated.

But the second oil price shock in 1979, combined with a sharp rise in world interest rates and the onset of a new recession in the West, brought the system to the verge of collapse. Developing countries could no longer pay their debts with their earnings from exports. Banks throughout the world faced calamitous losses, threatening cutbacks in lending to other customers, at home and abroad, and thus deepening the slump.

Strenuous efforts by the International Monetary Fund to force the banks to go on lending, and the debtor countries to retrench, have staved off disaster but represent only a temporary solution. World economic recovery, and with it the revival of international trade, is essential to resolving the debt crisis in the longer term. An extra 1 per cent on world growth, provided this is translated into additional trade, is worth 5 per cent off interest rates to developing nations.

In 1983, three main problems faced governments: how to achieve world recovery without reviving inflation; how to solve the international debt crisis; and how to stabilise exchange rates and make them more responsive to underlying economic conditions.

In an interdependent world, no one country can break from the herd. If others are pursuing contractionary policies, as many now are, a country like France which tries to expand its economy will find its balance of payments rapidly deteriorating as imports flood in with no compensating increase in exports. As a result, no country wants to be the first to reflate. But nor are they keen on reflating together, for fear of what might happen to inflation. The result is an unhappy stalemate in which those countries with strong currencies – mostly pursuing restrictive economic policies, with the United States a notable exception – in effect dictate to the rest of the world. Unless or until there is greater international consensus on underlying economic objectives, rectitude in financial affairs will be favoured by the currency markets, imparting a deflationary bias to the world economy as a whole.

On the debt crisis, too, the Western economies have been more eager to condemn developing countries for profligacy than to put in train moves towards economic expansion. The problems caused by high American interest rates and the strong dollar are generally recognised – but the will on the part of the Reagan administration to tackle the budget deficit which underpins them is singularly lacking.

Finally, there are increasing calls for international monetary reform, to reduce exchange rate volatility and misalignment.

There is now general agreement on the desirability of coordinated intervention to counter unwarranted short-term fluctuations. In addition, the leading industrial countries have pledged themselves to follow policies conducive to exchange rate stability.

The general idea is that if countries pursue similar policies, converging on low inflation, foreign exchange markets will have less to get their teeth into and more stable currencies will follow. The International Monetary Fund is already predicting that with inflation in the industrialised world down to its lowest level for 11 years, greater stability is in the offing.

Two nagging reservations remain. The first is that countries are under no obligation to pursue policies helpful to the rest of the world, especially where these conflict with domestic policy objectives, as the example of the United States demonstrates. The second is that greater convergence may not produce more stable exchange rates, since foreign exchange markets are sensitive not only to economic indicators but to political events and changes in preferences for currencies as well. That is why many people believe that it would be better to fix currency parities first and use that to enforce financial discipline on governments. The idea of moving towards target zones or guidelines for the dollar, yen and the European currencies is gaining ground.

These problems all impinge directly on Britain as an open trading nation with a reserve currency used in international trade. One of the lingering issues is whether Britain should become a full member of the European Monetary System, as a means of stabilising the pound. Now that oil prices are steady and revenues from the North Sea are expected to peak in the next couple of years, the argument that sterling's petro-currency status would disrupt the EMS is losing force. But concern that the pound is still too high against European currencies, especially the Deutschmark, and a lingering reluctance to surrender monetary autonomy, may keep Britain out for a while yet.

British industry's lack of competitiveness, combined with the economy's early move out of recession compared with the rest of the world, has led to a rapid worsening of the balance of payments, increasing pressure for restraints on trade. In 1983 Britain imported more manufactured goods than she exported for the first time since the Industrial Revolution two centuries ago. Import penetration in manufacturing has risen from 17 per cent of home demand in the early 1970s to 30 per cent today. The proportion of any *increase* in demand for manufactures may be as high as 50 per cent. There are now fears that, with oil revenues set to decline within a few years, the balance of payments could once again constrain the growth rate of the economy.

The first three pieces in this section deal with prospects for the global economy and its impact on the debt crisis. 'Make or break for the world economy' summarises the outlook as seen in autumn 1983. 'Recovery holds the key to third-world debt' explains why growth is crucial to overcome the international debt crisis. And 'Why the world wants a slow US recovery' looks at the interdependence of the world economy and the rôle of the US dollar and interest rates in promoting a sustained upswing. The next two articles focus on the dissatisfaction with floating exchange rates ('The growing disillusionment with floating exchange rates') and on proposals for reform ('In search of an anchor for floating currencies'). Finally, there are two pieces on international aspects of the British economy. 'The temptations of protectionism' discusses the pressures for protectionism and how the government is handling them. 'Missing the target on overseas investment' looks at what has happened to overseas investment since exchange controls were abolished in 1979 and argues that this has not damaged Britain's economy, though the policies which prompted that investment may have.

1 Make or break for the world economy

Published September 26 1983

The following article was published on the eve of the annual meeting of the International Monetary Fund and World Bank in Washington.

The coming year may well prove a make or break period for the world economy, now struggling to emerge from the most devastating recession for 50 years. At stake are the jobs of millions in the West; in much of the developing world the name of the game may be simple survival.

RECOVERY IN THE INDUSTRIAL COUNTRIES

Industrial production 1978 = 100 | Unemployment % | Inflation %

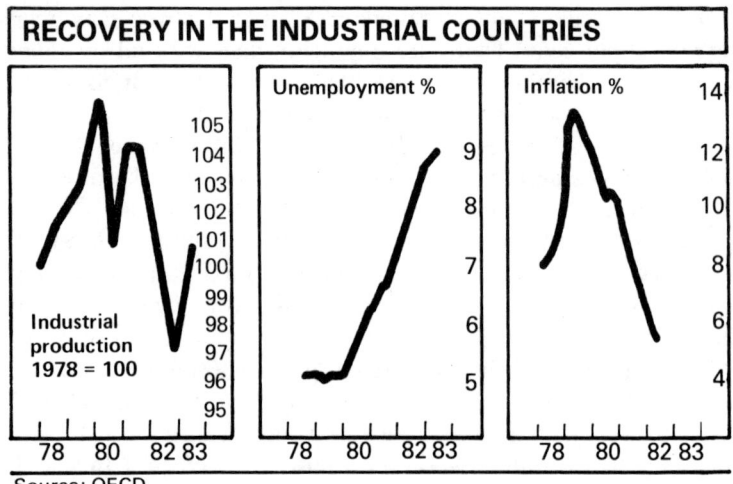

Source: OECD

'The situation may be one in which any departure from a path of modest growth would prove self-reinforcing', the Bank of England cautioned in its June 1983 *Quarterly Bulletin*. 'On the one hand, a strong upturn could gain momentum; but, were growth to falter now, a prolonged period of stagnation could ensue.'

Last year was the most dismal the global economy has experienced since the war. In the industrial countries output fell and unemployment climbed to a post-war peak. International trade dropped by 2.5 per cent, spreading recession throughout the world. In the developing countries, per capita incomes fell for the second successive year as their economies grew by a meagre 1.5 per cent, even less than the 2.5 per cent of 1981 and well below the 6 per cent or more annual growth typical of the 1970s.

In 1982 the economists of the International Monetary Fund, surveying the world scene, concluded gloomily that the industrial countries were stalled in a prolonged period of slow growth. When the dimensions of the international debt crisis became evident, after the Mexico débâcle that summer, the prospect of a global financial collapse looked all too possible.

The atmosphere this year, however, is one of cautious optimism. Output in the West is now thought to have touched bottom late last year, though outside North America the signs of recovery have been sporadic and feeble. The Organisation for Economic Cooperation and Development (OECD) is tentatively predicting growth in the industrial world of 2 per cent this year accelerating to 3.25 per cent in 1984. But these averages disguise a marked disparity between the United States (and to a lesser extent Japan) and the economies of Europe. The United States is already experiencing a robust recovery, which the OECD expects to average 3 per cent this year and 4.5 per cent in 1984. The Japanese economy is predicted to expand by 3.25 to 3.5 per cent over the same period – though this is well below the growth rates Japan is used to. But Europe is lagging well behind, with only the United Kingdom showing more than the weakest signs of recovery so far this year. The European economies are expected to grow by an anaemic 0.5 per cent in 1983 and only 1.5 per cent in 1984, nowhere near the 3 per cent or so needed to stop unemployment rising. By the end of next year 20 million people – some 12 per cent of the workforce – may be without jobs, two million more than today.

Nor is the present recovery by any means secure. It rests almost everywhere on higher consumer spending – resulting mainly from lower savings as falling inflation has helped to maintain the value of people's financial assets – and on a slowing or ending of the rundown of stocks by companies feeding through into factory production lines. But these factors can provide at best only a temporary stimulus to demand. If the recovery is to endure, there has to be a revival in capital investment. And here, as the OECD points out, the prospects are highly uncertain.

Business confidence, company profitability (and the expectations of future profits from investment), the cost of borrowing and the extent of existing spare capacity are all key influences on the willingness of industry to invest. While business confidence and profitability are looking up, real interest rates – after adjusting for inflation – are expected to remain at historically high levels and the rates of economic growth envisaged, especially in Europe, may not be adequate to eliminate spare capacity fast enough to make further investment seem worthwhile.

The doubts about investment are all the more worrying because the industrial countries can expect little stimulus from the rest of the world. The oil exporting countries have been forced by the drop in oil prices to cut back their purchases from the West. This has partly offset the beneficial impact of lower prices in cutting costly oil import bills.

Even greater retrenchment has been forced on many developing nations by the repercussions of the debt crisis. Net bank lending to the third world has shrivelled from $50,000m in 1981 to less than $10,000m at an annual rate in the fourth quarter of 1982, as the world's bankers have drawn in their horns to avoid further exposure to risk.

Leading Western governments, their central banks and the IMF are working overtime to keep credit lines to debtor nations open. But any increase in the flow of funds is likely to be swallowed up in debt repayments rather than used to increase imports from the industrial countries. What is more, this good work could be largely undone if, as many fear, American interest rates and the dollar remain at high levels or rise still further. With the bulk of the world's debt denominated in dollars and interest rates around the globe tied – tightly or loosely – to US rates, any upward movement could precipitate the very collapse governments are desperate to avert.

Without the ability to sell more goods to the West, to earn enough foreign exchange to repay debts and pay for imports needed for development, developing countries have no chance of digging themselves out of the economic mire. They are, as the IMF annual report makes clear, critically dependent on the progress of recovery in the industrial world and on the willingness of the West to keep their markets open to developing country imports. Growing protectionist pressures – provoked by rising joblessness – 'now present an additional obstacle to a renewal of growth in world trade and a hazard to the achievement of higher levels of output and productivity in the world economy', the IMF warns.

While the world's top international economists are at one in forecasting slow growth over the next couple of years they do not expect much if any further progress on inflation – now down to an eleven year low of 5 per cent in the industrial countries in the second quarter of 1983. Commodity prices, which in 1982 fell to their lowest level for 30 years, are expected to pick up as the recovery proceeds, though only gently, while firms are likely to take advantage of expanding demand to improve profit margins. But unit wage costs may well decline further as pay settlements ease and higher output boosts productivity growth. The OECD, in its *Economic Outlook* published in July 1983, expects the rise in unit labour costs to slow from 8 per cent in 1982 to 3–4 per cent this year and still less in 1984. Nevertheless inflation in the West is predicted to stick at around 6 per cent in 1984, little changed from today.

Within this general outlook for the world economy, the five biggest industrial countries face mixed fortunes. In the US, the linchpin of the global economic and financial system, rapid growth over the next couple of years, accompanied by a yawning trade deficit, is helping to create expanding markets for the rest of the world. But the benefits have been largely negated by high American interest rates and the strong dollar, which have forced other countries to pursue more contractionary policies to protect their currencies and avoid higher inflation.

The OECD expects the American recovery to continue throughout 1984, widening the external trade deficit to $35,000m – $40,000m (from $8,000m in 1982) and prompting a small increase in inflation from this year's low levels. But subsequent growth may well be dampened both by rising interest rates as Federal and private credit demands clash and by deflationary action after the Presidential elections in late 1984 to bring down the $200,000m Federal budget deficit.

Japan is likely to be the principal beneficiary of the American recovery. Its trade surplus is expected to rise to $35,000m in 1984 from $18,000m in 1982, in a mirror image of the American deficit. But little impetus is foreseen in the European economies which export much more to each other and to the Third World than they do to the United States.

Germany is resting its hopes for growth on a revival in investment, which would be an unprecedented development (investment normally lags behind an upturn in consumption). The OECD is predicting a 0.5 per cent increase in national output this year followed by 1.75 per cent in 1984, with unemployment stabilising at present high levels. Tight money and fiscal policies and the absence of a vigorous international upturn make a self-sustained recovery in Germany unlikely, the OECD comments gloomily.

In France, where the authorities have brought in tough austerity measures to reduce the gaping trade deficit, prospects are worse still, with the OECD foreseeing a drop of 0.5 per cent in GDP this year and only 0.5 per cent growth in 1984.

For Britain too the outlook is uncertain. The government, supported by the OECD, expects continued modest recovery in 1984, in the 2.25 to 2.5 per cent range[1], supported by higher

1 Treasury forecasts in November 1983 put growth in 1984 at 3 per cent, the same as in 1983.

118 *The International Scene*

investment and exports. This might be just enough to stop unemployment rising further. But, the OECD warns, 'the risks on the output projections would seem to be on the downside'.

The goal of sustained non-inflationary growth trumpeted by world leaders at the Williamsburg summit earlier this year looks as elusive as ever.

2 Recovery holds the key to third-world debt

Published February 2 1983

All analyses of the Third World's debt problems point to the same conclusion: no lasting solution is possible without global economic recovery. Its impact dwarfs anything that can be done by keeping credit lines open to countries in trouble or by strict economic adjustment policies by developing nations themselves.

Yet intense international activity to keep the cash flowing and put painful adjustment measures in place has not been matched by a similar determination to do something about growth. Without an increase in developing countries' export earnings, which depend essentially on expansion in world trade and activity, they will plunge deeper into debt. These earnings have been slashed by shrinking export markets in the industrial world and tumbling prices for the basic commodities they produce.

Exports by developing countries rose a meagre 1 per cent in 1982 compared with growth of 8 to 9 per cent a year in the second half of the 1970s. Meanwhile, commodity prices fell to their lowest levels in real terms for 30 years, with the result that their terms of trade – the ratio of export prices to import prices – deteriorated sharply.

The result has been to make the Third World debt burden virtually unsustainable. Contrary to popular belief, the majority of developing countries were not unduly profligate with cheap and easy credit before the recession set in. After the first oil price shock in 1973-74 they borrowed heavily to finance the massive balance of payments deficits needed to keep development programmes going with essential imports of oil, machinery and other goods.

But economic growth continued at a rapid pace, fuelled by rising exports. The ratio of total debt to exports for the main developing countries increased modestly from 120 per cent in 1975 to 133 per cent five years later, when it was on a downward trend. The ratio of total debt service (including short-term debt) to exports rose from 37 per cent in 1975 to 50 per cent in 1979 – a steeper increase but manageable.

Suddenly, debtor countries were hit from two directions. At the same time as the recession hit export earnings, the real value of their debts soared as world interest rates, propelled by the United States, reached new peaks. Between 1978 and 1981 interest rates doubled. The debt outstanding for the 21 biggest Third World borrowers rose to 170 per cent of their exports by the end of 1982 while the debt service ratio jumped from 50 per cent in 1979 to 75 per cent in 1982. Though interest rates have since eased, the outlook for world trade and so Third World export earnings remains bleak.

21 BIGGEST THIRD WORLD BORROWERS: DEBT/EXPORT RATIO*

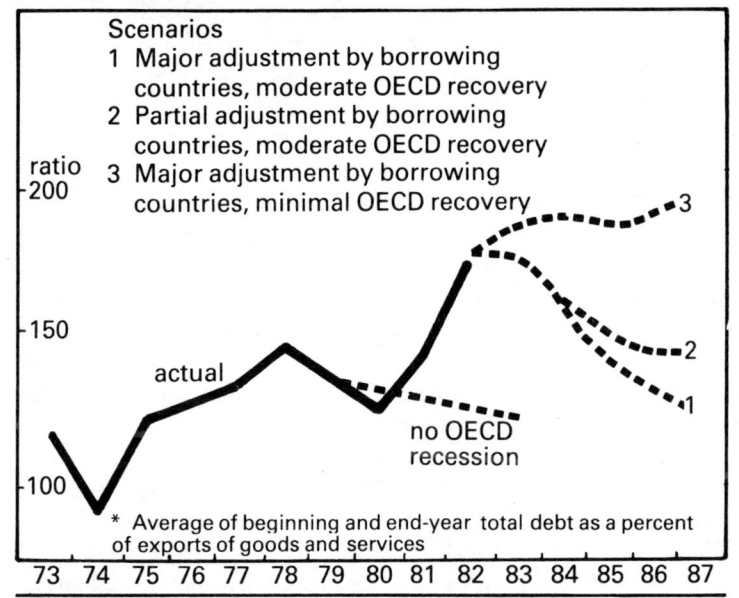

Scenarios
1 Major adjustment by borrowing countries, moderate OECD recovery
2 Partial adjustment by borrowing countries, moderate OECD recovery
3 Major adjustment by borrowing countries, minimal OECD recovery

* Average of beginning and end-year total debt as a percent of exports of goods and services

Source: Morgan Guaranty

Two recent studies of the world debt problem illustrate how serious the consequences of continued global recession could be. Morgan Guaranty, the American bank, has calculated that a minimal and delayed recovery in the industrial economies would mean bigger balance of payments deficits for developing countries even if they pursue resolute adjustment policies to curb demand and imports. 'Debt/export ratios would rise further. Financing needs would soar. Today's debt problems would only worsen' says Mr Rimmer de Vries, Senior Vice-President. A similar analysis by Data Resources Inc., an American independent forecasting group, which looked at the implications of three more years of recession, concluded that the international financial system might not have the resources to cope. Many more countries would join the small band of South American states where debts are at danger level – Mexico, Peru, Brazil, Chile and Argentina. 'Most developing countries would be in serious trouble by 1986 unless a steady world recovery materialises' the group reported. Their ability to finance economic development through borrowing would cease.

But the fact that world recovery is essential does not automatically bring it about. The OECD is expecting growth in the industrial countries of only 1.5 per cent this year, after a 0.5 per cent drop in 1982, picking up to 2.75 per cent by the first half of 1984.[1] This is feeble by past standards, partly because developing nations – which take a quarter of the West's exports – are being forced to cut back. Lower oil prices following the collapse of the OPEC cartel will help, boosting growth in the OECD area and reducing the financing needs of oil-importing developing countries. But there are serious downside risks too.

Forecasts of the upturn – repeatedly postponed – resemble nothing so much as a porcupine at bay, with the quills of predicted recovery sticking stiffly out of a declining rump of output. Failing business confidence and financing problems, for companies as well as the developing world, may hold back growth. So would a fresh surge in American interest rates, made increasingly likely by the Reagan administration's failure to cut record budget deficits. And the recrudescence of protectionist pressures may prevent the Third World from taking advantage of growing industrial markets.

1 In July 1983 it revised up its forecasts to 2 per cent growth in 1983 and 3.25 per cent in 1984.

A note of increasing desperation is thus creeping into calls, especially from bankers, for world reflation to stave off financial collapse. 'Passively awaiting spontaneous recovery of the global economy is both risky and wasteful', Mr de Vries says. In December 1982 he was one of the signatories to such a call from 26 economists under the auspices of the Washington-based Institute for International Economics.

Up to now the key industrial countries, including the United States and Britain, have put the fight against inflation first. There are signs that attitudes may be changing. But this has not been translated into deeds or even plans. Meanwhile, the risks to the world banking system from continuation of the slump remain grave. As Dr Johannes Witteveen, former managing director of the IMF and chairman of the prestigious Group of 30 international bankers and economists, said in October 1982: 'You cannot have a healthy financial or banking system in the middle of a sick economy.'

3 Why the world wants a slow US recovery

Published May 18 1983

The United States is expected to stage a distinctly anaemic economic recovery this year. The administration is predicting growth of 4.7 per cent over the course of 1983, comfortably within the 4 to 5 per cent consensus of most outside forecasters. This compares with upswings of 6 or 7 per cent typical of previous post-war recoveries.

Yet far from finding this disconcerting, those charged with the management of the American economy are rubbing their hands with quiet satisfaction. They positively want a slow recovery and they hope it will continue that way. Too rapid growth, they argue, would run the risk of triggering a fresh bout of inflation, forcing the authorities to bring the upturn to an untimely end. More immediately, it would threaten a sharp rise in interest rates as heavy borrowing by companies to finance stocks and

US INDICATORS

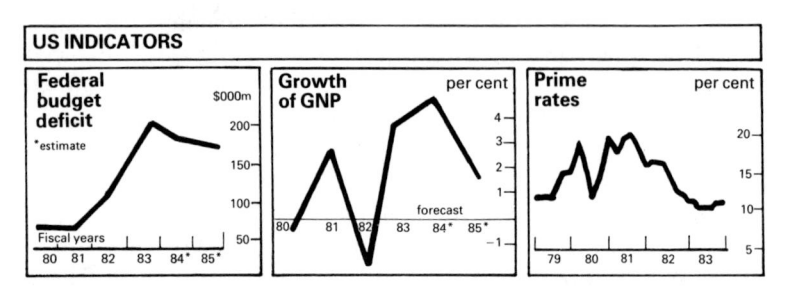

Federal budget deficit $000m — Fiscal years 80, 81, 82, 83, 84*, 85* (*estimate)

Growth of GNP per cent — 80, 81, 82, 83, 84*, 85* (forecast)

Prime rates per cent — 79, 80, 81, 82, 83

Sources: Simon & Coates, Morgan Guaranty

investment clashed with the huge credit demands of the Federal government. Economic indicators published in the past week or so suggesting the upswing may be stronger than predicted have thus been greeted with some dismay.

At the root of the sluggish rise in activity lies the chillingly high level of US interest rates, for which the massive and growing federal budget deficit is held chiefly responsible. From a deficit of $58,000m in 1981, President Reagan's first year in office, the budget gap has quadrupled to an estimated $210,000m in the current fiscal year, with deficits of $200,000m plus projected, on present policies, 'as far as the eye can see'. This would lead to a doubling of the national debt within five years.

It is not the deficits this year and next that cause most concern. Without them the recovery would be even more feeble than it is. It is that there seems no prospect of lower deficits two years out and more, when recovery should be well under way. Fears of the resulting credit crunch have kept long-term interest rates at punitively high levels despite the deep recession. This has depressed investment. And, by pushing up the value of the dollar to grossly uncompetitive levels, it has hurt exports and ensured that much of the benefit of higher home demand is syphoned abroad as imports are sucked in.

In the past a sub-normal upswing in the United States would cause considerable heartache in the rest of the world which has traditionally relied on this giant economy to stoke the engines of global activity. Times have changed. World growth prospects now depend at least as much, if not more, on what happens to US interest rates and the dollar as they do on US growth.

Recovery in one country is transmitted to the rest of the world through trade. Though the United States remains the world's biggest single trading nation, Germany and Japan together are even more important. And the European Community as a whole does twice as much trade as the US. Expansion in Europe and Japan, however, is inhibited by high American interest rates and the strong dollar, which have forced countries to adopt tight money policies to stem capital outflows and limit the inflationary consequences of their falling currencies. The OECD recently calculated that a 10 per cent depreciation of the dollar, accompanied by a cut of 2 percentage points in interest rates in the industrial countries, would boost OECD output by more than 1 per cent. This compares with a boost to OECD output of 0.25 per cent or less for every 1 per cent of growth in the United States.

Equally important is the expanding rôle of developing countries in the world economy. Two-thirds of their exports (including those of OPEC) go to the industrial countries. One quarter of OECD exports go to the poorer nations. Growth of 1 per cent in the developing countries adds 0.25 per cent to activity in the industrialised world, rivalling the impact of the American economy in driving or depressing international recovery. Indeed, the potential impact of developing countries may be greater. In the 1970s their economies grew nearly twice as fast as the 3 per cent a year registered by the US. That could well be repeated if world recovery takes hold.

But the most dynamic of the developing countries are now heavily, sometimes dangerously, in debt – to the tune of more than $700,000m. Most of this debt is denominated and serviced in dollars. Each 1 per cent drop in US interest rates is reckoned to wipe $4,000m off annual debt servicing costs, while a fall in the dollar would make repayments easier to meet from non-dollar export earnings. It would also ease the pressure for trade protection in the United States which threatens to cut off vital export markets for many developing countries.

Reduction in the debt servicing burden is crucial if debtor countries are to expand their imports from the rich nations and renew the rapid economic growth which austerity measures forced on them by world recession and the debt crisis have brought abruptly to a halt. Any rise in American interest rates could prove disastrous for growth in the developing world, with dismal repercussions in the West. Thus in the short term, while the US budget deficit problem remains unresolved, the world as well as the US will have to hope that the smouldering American recovery does not catch fire.

In the longer term, as Western leaders meeting shortly in Williamsburg will impress forcibly upon President Reagan, failure to put the deficit on a credibly declining path threatens to shipwreck any recovery, modest or otherwise, in the US and the rest of the world.

The American recovery did in fact prove more robust than the forecasters predicted, with growth of about 6 per cent expected over the course of 1983. Interest rates rose slightly, though by less than many had feared. But the shadow of the federal deficit continued to overhang the currency and money markets, keeping the dollar strong and stopping interest rates from falling despite a further drop in inflation.

4 The growing disillusionment with floating exchange rates

Published November 1 1982

The experience of the world financial system since the collapse in 1971 of the Bretton Woods agreement on fixed exchange rates has not been a happy one. Disillusionment with floating currencies is growing; supporters of world monetary reform are both more numerous and more outspoken.

When the rigid structure of Bretton Woods disintegrated under the weight of accelerating world-wide inflation and growing and volatile international capital flows, the adherents of floating rates were quick to seize the intellectual advantage. Floating, they said, would allow currencies to adjust smoothly to underlying changes in economic circumstances, so that countries could avoid the dislocation of trade and capital flows produced by infrequent big exchange rate shifts. It would automatically eliminate balance of payments problems, enabling countries to pursue expansionary domestic policies without external constraints. It would cut individual countries loose from the obligation to run their economies in step with the dominant trading nations in order to maintain fixed parities, giving them greater autonomy to run their affairs as they wished. And it would release them in particular from the constricting financial hegemony of the United States, whose original commitment to peg the dollar to a fixed gold price underpinned the Bretton Woods system.

These claims look faintly incredible now. Not only have currencies been unprecedentedly volatile since floating began; far from offsetting changes in domestic costs and prices, and smoothing adjustment to structural developments in trade patterns and so on, they have all too often gone against them. Real exchange rates – adjusted for changes in domestic costs – have shown dramatic shifts. The real value of the pound is now 40 per cent above its 1975 level (only part of which can be explained by possession of North Sea oil). The real value of the dollar is nearly 30 per cent higher than in 1975 while the yen has swung from an appreciation of more than 20 per cent to a drop of about 12 per cent from 1975 levels within two years.

Persistently out-of-line exchange rates exacerbate countries' economic troubles and damage international relationships. If, as in Britain's case, the currency is clearly over-valued the result is to destroy competitiveness and produce rapid de-industrialisation. If, like Japan, the exchange rate is under-valued, the result is to boost the export sector at the expense of domestic consumers, which has led to increasingly bitter trade rows and a growing climate of protectionism.

Many people now believe that foreign exchange markets by themselves simply cannot ensure that currencies adjust to fundamental economic factors, even in the longer run. With exchange rates influenced not only by what is happening now but by expectations of future developments and policy responses to them, market operators are forced to interpret a barrage of constantly changing confusing and contradictory signals.

As the influential Group of 30 top international bankers and economists pointed out in a report published in May 1982 'exchange rate expectations seem to be loosely held, strongly influenced by current events and subject to "band-wagon" effects. It is possible that with more experience of floating rates market operators will learn to take a longer term view, but we

REAL EFFECTIVE EXCHANGE RATES 1975-79 = 100

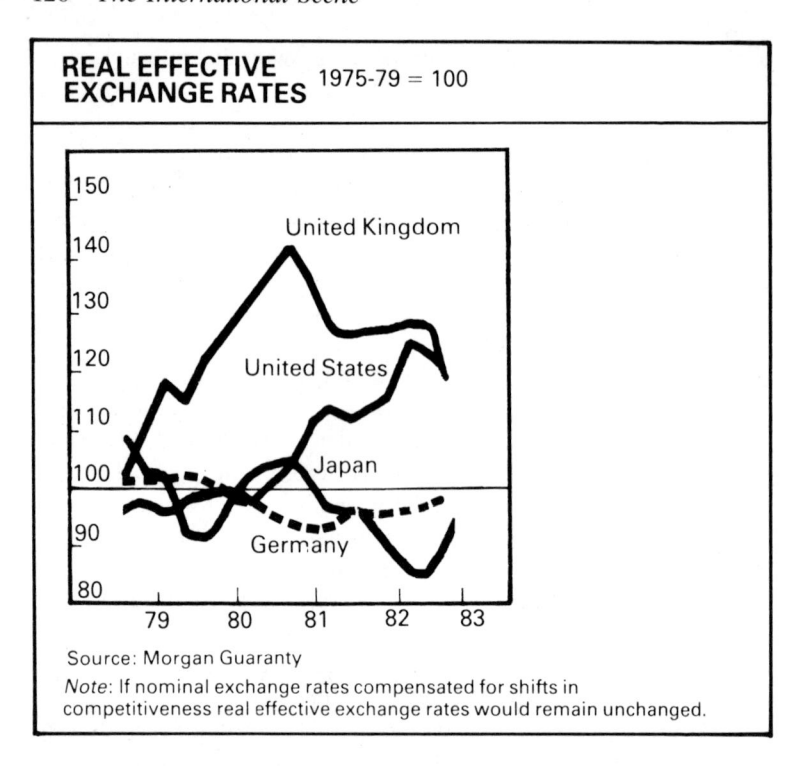

[Chart showing real effective exchange rates from 1979 to 1983 for United Kingdom, United States, Japan, and Germany]

Source: Morgan Guaranty

Note: If nominal exchange rates compensated for shifts in competitiveness real effective exchange rates would remain unchanged.

are not very optimistic about this.'

The other hopes of the free-floaters have also been disappointed. Since floating began two oil price shocks and the burgeoning development of international capital markets have produced the biggest payments imbalances the world has ever seen. Countries found that in practice their freedom to pursue independent economic policies was tightly circumscribed by the reaction, often exaggerated, of the foreign exchange markets.

Furthermore, America's dominance of the world financial scene is undiminished. High and fluctuating United States interest rates in the past three years or so, and the consequent movement of the dollar, have been the overriding factor on foreign exchange markets and a principal cause of the prolonged world recession. The desire to escape the damaging consequences of currency instability led early on to attempts to establish a stable currency zone in Europe. The first such attempt, the 'snake', set up in 1972 had a chequered and not altogether successful history.

Its successor, the European Monetary System, which began

early in 1979, has so far proved more robust. Currencies in the EMS fluctuate against each other within narrow limits, and parity changes can only be made with the agreement of all the members.

The objects of the EMS were two-fold: to reduce exchange rate volatility to provide a stable framework for trade and industry within the European Community; and to establish greater convergence of member economies by imposing on them the discipline of maintaining fixed parities. In the first the EMS has been remarkably successful. A recent study by Simon and Coates, the city stockbrokers, found that intra-EMS volatility had been roughly half that of similar cross-rates outside the system. On the other hand, fluctuations against the dollar were just as great as for non-member currencies. And convergence of economic performance, especially on inflation, looks as far away as ever.

Though the French have latterly toned down their expansionary policies to restrain inflation and defend the franc, fundamental differences between French and German approaches and circumstances increasingly threaten EMS stability. Realignments have become both more frequent and more extensive. Any recovery by the Deutschmark against the dollar, which would drag up weaker currencies in its wake, could place the EMS under intolerable strain.

Britain did not become a full member of the EMS in 1979 chiefly because the Callaghan government feared that this would prevent the pound falling which was needed to preserve competitiveness. In the event, sterling soared on a tide of North Sea oil and the high interest rates produced by Mrs Thatcher's tough money policies. EMS membership would not necessarily have prevented the pound from rising as it did. Britain might have been forced to apply for repeated revaluation or leave the EMS altogether. And the government might well have jibbed at deliberately running more expansionary policies to keep sterling down when the defeat of inflation was its principal objective. On the other hand, the reduced volatility of the pound against European currencies might have helped industry, which sends more than 40 per cent of its exports to the Community, to plan ahead and cut the cost of hedging currency risks.

Proposals for world monetary reform are now coming thick and fast. At one end of the spectrum are the Group of 30's modest proposals for concerted official intervention to stop currencies getting grossly out of line with economic circumstances (what the Governor of the Bank of England has called a helpful hand on the tiller), and for more regard to be paid, especially by the United States, to the international implications of domestic policies. At the other end are calls, by Lord Lever and others, for a return to a system of fixed but adjustable parities policed by the International Monetary Fund or some other supra-national body. However, without the backing of the United States, which still clings staunchly to free market ideals and its policy of 'benign neglect' in the currency arena, attempts at reform stand little chance of success.

5 In search of an anchor for floating currencies

Published May 25 1983

'Nothing would show the ordinary people of western democracies more clearly that we are emerging from crisis into a more predictable and safer world than the joint announcement of the will gradually to restore a system based on fixed exchange rates', M Valery Giscard d'Estaing, former President of France, wrote last week, describing his hopes for the Williamsburg summit. He will be disappointed. No such announcement is on the cards. But the signs are that, ten years after the Bretton Woods regime of fixed exchange rates finally broke down, world leaders are yearning for something better than the freely floating system which succeeded it, and are receptive to proposals for change.

Since 1973 – when attempts to patch up Bretton Woods were abandoned – world growth has been slower, inflation higher and international financial conditions more unstable than at any time for half a century. The critics of floating rates argue that this is no coincidence. Instead of cushioning shocks, like the oil price hikes of 1973-74 and 1979, the floating system has amplified them, they say. Instead of adjusting smoothly to levels determined by relative competitiveness, currencies have lurched from one extreme to the next and are as likely to exacerbate economic difficulties as compensate for them. Instead of greater freedom to

TRADE-WEIGHTED EXCHANGE RATES

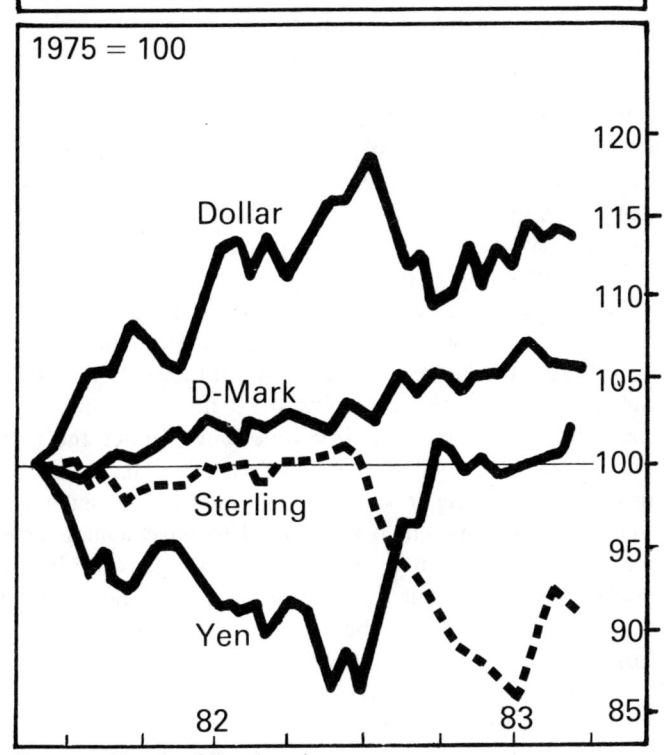

1975 = 100

Source: Bank of England

conduct economic policy, free of the balance of payments constraint imposed by a fixed exchange rate, governments have found themselves at the mercy of massive and unpredictable financial flows. Instead of liberation from American dominance of the international financial system the dollar remains the uncrowned king – and a baleful ruler it has proved to be.

Since 1979, when the United States central bank – the Federal Reserve Board – brought in tight control of the money supply, and interest rates and the dollar went through the roof, calls for reform of the floating rate system have been gathering pace. Until recently those calls have found little echo in the minds of the Reagan administration, which has stuck rigidly to its policy of 'benign neglect' of the dollar and belief in the ultimate rightness of the market in determining the currency's value. Now, however, there are signs that the US may be willing to budge, at least a little.

The dollar's overvaluation is hurting the American economy because US goods are being priced out of world markets and because debt-ridden developing countries can no longer afford to buy goods from abroad, the US included. In addition, as pressures mount within the United States for protection against imports, American government officials are beginning to worry about the threat to the international trading system posed by currency misalignments. In particular they, and others, point to the undervalued yen as an important cause of Japan's phenomenal and threatening export performance, which has provoked increasing restraints on Japanese goods coming to the West.

The fixed rate system, economists point out, made financial flows subordinate to trade flows. If trade did not balance countries ran a payments surplus or deficit, with private and official capital flows moving to compensate. Under the floating system trade has become subordinate to financial flows. Countries are putting restraints on trade to offset financial imbalances, restraints which are bound to have damaging long-term repercussions on investment and growth. This will hurt their economies far more than restrictions on capital flows, however inconvenient the latter may be.

Proposed reforms to the international currency system essentially fall into three categories, in ascending order of ambition. First, there are calls for greater intervention by governments to buy and sell currencies on the foreign exchange markets to dampen excessive short-term fluctuations in rates. A report commissioned after the 1982 Versailles summit found that intervention was effective in stabilising currencies, especially if it was reinforced by changes in monetary policy such as interest rates, and if it was co-ordinated with other countries. This report was endorsed by finance ministers from the seven summit countries,[1] including the United States, in Washington last month, when they announced their willingness to undertake co-ordinated intervention. Intervention can brake currency swings and may make speculators think twice. But, as the French quickly discovered, it is powerless against determined market pressure. The sources of that pressure have to be tackled directly.

1 The United States, Japan, Germany, France, the United Kingdom, Canada and Italy.

The second set of proposals, backed by Sir Geoffrey Howe, the Chancellor, and most of the international financial establishment, look to increasing convergence and co-ordination of national economic policies as the route to more stable exchange rates. Some progress has already been made. The Versailles summit agreed that for the first time the five countries which make up the currencies of the special drawing right – the reserve currency of the International Monetary Fund – should from time to time meet M Jacques de Larosiere, the Fund's managing director, to look at each other's policies and their impact on the world economic and financial system.

Since Versailles, the group – the US, Britain, France, Germany and Japan – have met three times and by all accounts the exchanges have been frank, with the US in particular coming under fire for failing to control swelling budget deficits which are keeping interest rates and the dollar high. These arrangements, by common consent, are likely to be strengthened at Williamsburg. But though their supporters believe that progress towards low inflation, with France now falling into line, may already be ushering in an era of more stable currencies there is still plenty of divergence – notably in interest rates – for the fickle markets to seize upon.

That is why, for many, a third option – a return to a system of fixed exchange rates – seems to be the only solution to both volatility and misalignment. President Mitterrand, in his dramatic call this month for a new Bretton Woods conference, more or less implied that world economic salvation depended on it. Most of the advocates of a fixed exchange rate system have in mind the setting of target zones rather than exact parities for the three major currency blocs – the dollar, the Europeans (including sterling) and the yen. Countries would undertake to manage their economies to maintain their currencies within the zones, and would adjust policy and intervene in the markets to defend them.

But central bankers and the majority of the summit countries remain sceptical. They do not like the idea of subordinating economic policy to a single exchange rate objective, nor are they confident of their ability to keep the markets at bay. In deference to President Mitterrand, however, the Western leaders may well agree to study further ways of moving towards more stable and sensible exchange rates. An international monetary conference – albeit years rather than months ahead – is by no means ruled out.

The summit heads of government agreed to ask finance ministers to study ways of improving the international monetary system 'and to consider the part which might, in due course, be played in this process by a high level monetary conference'.

6 The temptations of protectionism

Published November 5 1982

A great deal of hypocrisy is talked about trade protection in Britain. When news that the Cabinet was considering import curbs surfaced recently, reaction ranged from applause from those who believe this country is being done down by sticking to free trade rules no one else is observing to antagonism from those who see the path of righteousness being abandoned for protectionist perfidy.

In truth, Britain has been putting up the shutters against free entry of imports steadily since the mid-1970s, in common with the rest of the industrialised world. Nearly half her total trade is covered by restrictions, not counting tariffs, according to the National Institute of Economic and Social Research. For manufactured goods the proportion has jumped from virtually nothing to at least 13 per cent since 1974, only marginally below the EEC average of 14 per cent and 15 per cent for the industrial nations taken together.

The sudden re-emergence of import controls as a big political issue arises because several concerns troubling ministers have come to a head at roughly the same time. Of these by far the most important is the growing penetration of British markets by imports, which means that the benefit of higher demand in the economy is increasingly being snatched by foreign suppliers. In the manufacturing sector, which is most exposed to foreign competition, about half of any increase in demand now goes on imports. Since the trough of the recession was reached in spring 1981, demand in the economy has risen by some 3 per cent. But

The International Scene 133

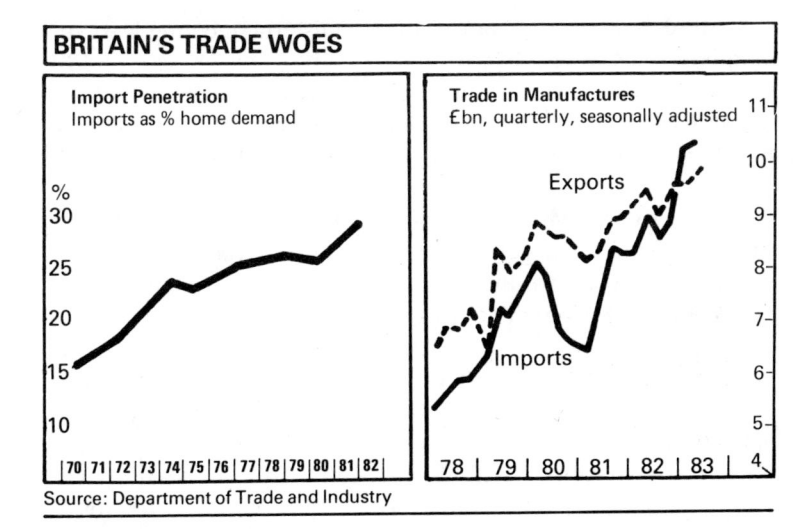

BRITAIN'S TRADE WOES

Import Penetration — Imports as % home demand (1970–1982), rising from about 15% to about 30%.

Trade in Manufactures — £bn, quarterly, seasonally adjusted (1978–1983), showing Exports and Imports both rising from around 5 to around 10.

Source: Department of Trade and Industry

industrial production is less than 1 per cent up, and when North Sea activities are excluded production has actually fallen slightly. This places government in great difficulty. It means that a large increase in domestic demand is needed to produce a small pickup in output and jobs, exacerbating the risks of economic expansion for both inflation and the balance of payments.

James Capel, the stockbrokers, estimated recently that to push unemployment down to two million, national output would need to be about 10 per cent greater than it is now. This would imply an unsustainable balance of payments deficit of between £5bn and £10bn.

A related factor is the prolongation of the world recession which has intensified international competition for shrinking markets and triggered moves to protectionism by developing and developed countries alike. British industry, already suffering a competitive handicap from the high value of the pound, has found itself increasingly squeezed at home and abroad, while facing additional obstacles in exporting to traditional markets or attempting to penetrate new ones.

In the past few weeks alone the government has been obliged, with its EEC partners, to accept a voluntary restraint agreement on steel exports to the United States; France has brought in a series of measures designed deliberately to make life more difficult for importers; and Canada and Australia have stepped up their import barriers.

A third factor is the approaching ministerial meeting later this month of the General Agreement on Tariffs and Trade (GATT), the first such meeting for nine years. This has inevitably led to a reappraisal of how the world trading system is working from Britain's point of view, and focussed attention on areas of grievance.

Britain, along with other industrial countries, is particularly irritated by the privileged status of the more advanced developing countries, such as South Korea and Brazil, now quite sophisticated industrial economies. Their exports still come in to Britain duty-free, or nearly so, while British exports to them face huge protective tariff walls. For instance, biscuit exports to Brazil attract a 185 per cent tariff (not to mention a temporary import ban) while biscuit imports to the EEC pay duty of 13 per cent. Cars imported from South Korea come to Europe duty-free, subject to a quota, while cars exported to Korea have 100 to 150 per cent tariffs slapped on, plus a special excise tax.

Ministers have also been brought face to face with evident trade inequities by two recent events: the threatened blacking by the transport union of imports of the Vauxhall Corsa from Spain (tariff here only 4.2 per cent compared with 36.7 per cent for car exports to Spain); and the Prime Minister's visit to Japan, which ended with few if any positive measures to reduce the enormous trade imbalance between the two countries.

The result has been to make the government determined to use what muscle it has to secure 'equitable market access' for British exports, including the possible use of retaliatory import curbs. True to its free market convictions, the government remains committed to the general principle (if not always the fine print) of free trade, despite pressure from the strong protectionist wing of the Conservative party. The Trade Minister, Mr Peter Rees, said last week that the government's object was not to limit free trade but to extend it. 'We are pressing for greater liberalisation, with possible retaliatory measures as a last resort', he insisted.

But whatever the intent behind import controls the effects will be the same. If efforts to bring down barriers abroad fail, and Britain is forced to carry through threats to impose restrictions of her own, the result is likely to be self-defeating. Export markets will shrivel as countries strike back or find themselves with less foreign earnings to buy British goods. Prices will rise as low-cost imports are replaced – on past experience – with high-cost imports or import substitutes. Real incomes will fall. The impact on home production and jobs will be adverse rather than beneficial.

The government would do far better to strike directly at where the problems lie: to use whatever diplomatic pressure it can bring to bear, preferably with others, on offending countries short of committing itself to damaging retaliatory controls; and to play its part in improving the competitiveness of British industry, above all by acceding to a fall in the damagingly high exchange rate.

7 Missing the target on overseas investment

Published January 31 1983

'What does it profit a man to have a pension paid from Japan if he spends half his life in Britain on the dole?' So Mr Peter Shore, Labour's Shadow Chancellor, demanded of leaders of British pension funds a year or so ago. With this rhetorical flourish he encapsulated the case of Labour and the trade unions against the huge and rising flood of investment overseas.

The case is simply put. Every pound sent abroad is money which could have been spent in Britain, improving the efficiency and profitability of industry at home and boosting output and jobs. Instead, it is going to strengthen other countries' economies, depriving British workers of employment and sapping the ability of industry to meet international competition. Thus it is with mounting disquiet that Mr Shore and his colleagues view the surge in outward investment that has followed the government's abolition of exchange controls in October 1979.

Direct investment by companies in their overseas operations nearly doubled between 1979 and 1981, before tailing off in 1982. But portfolio investment – investment in overseas stocks and shares – which was severely inhibited by controls has soared. Since 1979 flows abroad have increased five-fold and show no sign of abating. Some City estimates suggest that total long-term outflows are now running close to £1bn a month, three times 1979 levels.

Do these outflows damage the interests of British workers? For direct investment the answer is probably no. The cash goes to finance the overseas activities of British firms, not their rivals, and what studies there are suggest that investment abroad does not divert cash from profitable projects in Britain. Much direct investment goes to strengthen overseas distribution or supply networks or is in countries which restrict British exports or where the order would otherwise go to a foreign competitor with consequent loss of markets to Britain. On balance, the evidence points to a boost to exports and jobs rather than the reverse.

The arguments put up in defence of portfolio investment are more tenuous. The first is that a large part of the jump in overseas investment represents a once-for-all adjustment to abolition of exchange controls as financial institutions rearrange their portfolios with a higher proportion of foreign assets. Once achieved, it is argued, the flows needed to maintain that proportion will be much smaller. However, there is little sign so far of any easing.

The second is that channelling funds abroad has not affected investment in British company securities. In 1979, for instance, UK pension funds invested 41 per cent of their new money in government stock, 27 per cent in company shares and 8 per cent in overseas securities. In 1981 the share of overseas investment had jumped to 23 per cent. But the proportion going on UK company shares was slightly higher while the proportion going on gilts had slumped to 27 per cent.[1] If investment abroad had been restricted, financial institutions might have invested more in British companies – but they might equally well have put more cash into gilts or short-term assets.

Finally, it is argued that investment abroad has directly benefited British industry by keeping the exchange rate lower than it would otherwise have been (though interest rates have been slightly higher too). The present government has welcomed overseas investment for this reason, because it helps to offset the impact of North Sea oil on the value of the pound and provides assets which will go on producing income after North Sea oil has run out.

The same objectives could have been achieved differently,

1 For later figures see table.

THE GROWTH OF OVERSEAS INVESTMENT

Direct | Portfolio (£m, 78–83)

Source: CSO

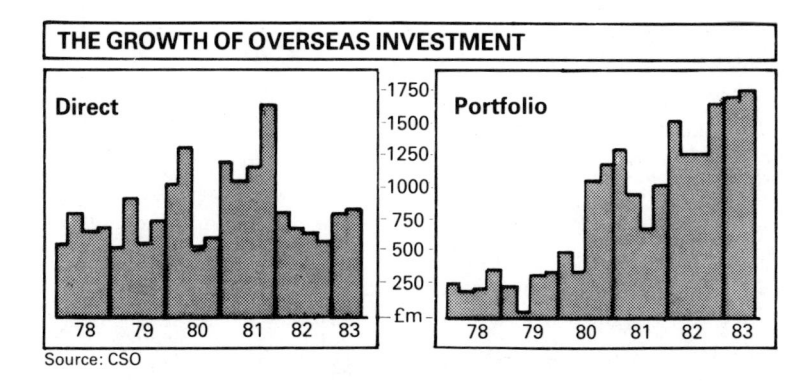

however. There is no reason in principle why the build-up of assets from the proceeds of North Sea oil has to be abroad rather than at home. The government chose to run tight money and budget policies which, by driving up interest rates and producing a huge balance of payments surplus, pushed up the exchange rate. This has squeezed domestic profitability, making investment at home less attractive, and cheapened the cost of foreign assets which have become much more attractive. But if ministers had been willing to pursue more expansionary economic policies this would both have kept sterling down and independently boosted output and jobs.

The level of overseas portfolio investment is a function of the government's approach to economic management, and it is official policies that must be judged rather than the behaviour of the financial institutions. There is no evidence that investment in Britain is being curtailed by a shortage of cash. The real investment problem in this country is not lack of funds but lack of profitable opportunities. Low investment is as much a symptom of Britain's deeper economic *malaise* of poor competitiveness and profitability as a cause of it.

For long-term capital flows, the argument for reinstatement of exchange controls is a weak one. The much stronger argument in favour of controls on short-term speculative flows is often neglected. The existence of massive footloose funds swishing about the world in search of the highest return makes the task of government immensely more difficult. Its ability to pursue coherent domestic economic policies is seriously impaired by swings in the exchange rate or in money growth which may bear little relation to underlying economic conditions or to the

Where new investment went

	Overseas investments £m	%	UK company shares £m	%	UK government stock £m	%
Insurance companies						
1979	93	2	685	15	2541	57
1980	566	11	743	15	2176	43
1981	801	13	924	15	2207	36
1982	1242	19	1620	25	1841	28
1983 (1st half)	744	22	651	19	1105	33
Pension funds						
1979	459	8	1503	27	2294	41
1980	1459	23	2180	34	2083	32
1981	1608	23	1887	28	1873	27
1982	1941	29	1952	29	1283	19
1983 (1st half)	889	23	761	20	942	25

Source: CSO, *Financial Statistics*

country's needs. The trouble is that these short-term funds are the most difficult to regulate. Exchange controls certainly did not prevent recurrent sterling crises, nor did they stop the pound rising from 1977 as the North Sea oil factor came into play.

But there are economists who believe that abandoning them altogether may have increased the risk of turbulence and removed a weapon, however flimsy, that might help. They can turn to Keynes for support. In a paragraph which has some relevance today he wrote in the early 1940s:

> 'There is no country which can, in future, safely allow the flight of funds for political reasons or to evade domestic taxation or in anticipation of the owner turning refugee. Equally, there is no country that can safely receive fugitive funds which cannot safely be used for fixed investment and might turn it into a surplus country against its will and contrary to the real facts.'[1]

1 J. M. Keynes, 'Proposals for an International Currency (or Clearing) Union' quoted in Sir Alec Cairncross, *Control of Long-term International Capital Movements*, Brookings Institution, 1973.

Discussion Questions

Section 1

1. To what extent did the government reflate the economy during the period 1981-83? Why did it not reflate further?
2. How have interest rates been affected by the government's monetary and social policies?
3. Why is the provision of public services threatened by current economic trends?
4. To what extent is the present level of government borrowing contractionary?
5. How, why and to what extent did the 1979-83 government cut taxes?
6. Why might it be undesirable to cut the nationalised industries? planned investment expenditures? Can privatisation solve the problem of financing this investment?

Section 2

1. How has the reduction in the rate of inflation been achieved?
2. What opportunities has North Sea oil created within the economy? How have these been used?
3. In what ways has the government tried to promote economic growth
4. What are the major reasons for public expenditure cuts having proved difficult? What are the implications of slow rates of economic growth for public expenditure?
5. Can the size of the black economy be estimated? Are efforts to reduce it likely to benefit the economy?

Section 3

1. Why has the economic cost of the government's fight against inflation proved to be higher than expected?
2. 'High unemployment is caused by inflation.' 'Falling unemployment leads to higher inflation.' Are these statements consistent?
3. Why is inflation electorally unpopular? What reasons are there to believe that it could accelerate again?

4. Why have policies designed to deal with unemployment enjoyed such limited success?
5. Can the natural rate of unemployment be reduced by changing the level of unemployment benefit?
6. Do official figures give an accurate representation of the level of unemployment?
7. To what extent do special unemployment measures actually alleviate the problems of a) youth unemployment, and b) the long-term unemployed?
8. Could an economic forum help to control inflation?

Section 4

1. Can the recent improvements in productivity levels be sustained? Why is productivity growth seen as being essential to the health of the economy?
2. To what extent does the competitiveness of UK products depend on productivity levels?
3. How have a) private investment, and b) total investment, varied over the past decade?
4. Can lower interest rates create an expansionary trend in the economy?
5. What factors influence the government's exchange rate policy?

Section 5

1. What consequences follow from the greater interdependence of the world's economies?
2. How does the level of economic activity in the US affect other economies?
3. How have floating exchange rates functioned in practice?
4. What are the possible alternatives to a system of floating exchange rates?
5. To what extent has UK trade policy drifted away from the principle of free trade in recent years?
6. How do international capital movements affect countries' balance of payments?
7. What are the arguments for and against maintaining exchange controls? What has been the effect of removing them?